Cupcakes, Cupcakes, & More Cupcakes!
~~~~~~~~~~~~~~~~~~~~~~~~~~

An Imagine Book
Published by Charlesbridge
85 Main Street, Watertown, MA 02472
617-926-0329
www.charlesbridge.com

Created by Penn Publishing Ltd.
1 Yehuda Halevi Street, Tel Aviv, Israel 65135
www.penn.co.il

Design: Michal & Dekel
Layout: Ariane Rybski

Library of Congress
Catalog-in-Publication Data Available

ISBN 978-1-936140-43-5

2 4 6 8 10 9 7 5 3

Manufactured in China, January 2013

For information about custom editions, special sales, premium and corporate purchases,
please contact Charlesbridge Publishing at specialsales@charlesbridge.com

Cupcakes, Cupcakes, & More Cupcakes!

~~~~~~

Lilach German

Photography by Danya Weiner

imagine!
Publishing

Contents

~~~~~~~~~~~~~~~~~~~

Introduction
6

Cupcake Essentials
8

The Classics, Cupcake Style
20

Cupcakes for Kiddies
46

Cupcake Celebrations
66

A Cupcake to Your Health
84

Cupcakes for Connoisseurs
112

Conversion Charts
140

Index
142

Introduction

The traditional American cupcake, which was developed at the beginning of the 19th century, is actually a personal cake. While it's similar to the muffin, cupcakes are usually covered in rich buttercream in an array of colors, and imaginatively decorated. The term "cupcake" has two meanings: One refers to the small size and shape of the cakes, which at one time were baked in actual cups, including teacups. Another meaning refers to the practice of measuring ingredients by cups rather than by weight, as they had been in the past. The preparation of the cupcake was considered revolutionary in its time for a number of reasons. To begin with, baking time was significantly reduced (especially in comparison with the large cakes once baked). In addition, much time was saved through the use of uniform measuring tools for all ingredients.

Many people tend to confuse the muffin and the cupcake; so let's consider the difference. The cupcake is a personal cake baked in muffin tins, while the muffin, in the classic sense of the word, refers to a kind of bun (for instance, the English muffin) that can be sweet or savory, yet certainly comes under the category of bread, not cake. An additional distinction refers to the different method of preparation. When preparing muffins, two separate mixtures of dry ingredients and wet ingredients are combined and oil, rather than butter, is used. Cupcakes, on the other hand, are small cakes prepared by whipping butter and sugar with the eggs, resulting in an airier and softer texture than that found in muffins. The manner of decorating is different as well; cupcakes arrive frosted and glazed in rich creams.

Without a doubt, the personal cupcake has enjoyed a renaissance in recent years and is popular among children and adults alike. In my opinion, the reason for the cupcake's popularity stems not only from the ease of preparation and its personal size, but also because its look can be easily changed to suit individual tastes. When it comes to cupcakes, the range of recipes one can find and create is truly limitless.

In this book, I've divided the recipes into six central topics in order to allow for easier location of your preferred recipe. I encourage you to use one of the basic recipes and "dress" it with imaginative decorations according to occasion and inspiration.

Cupcake Essentials

Equipment
~~~~~~

Most of the necessary cupcake tools are basic and can be found in the average kitchen, while some of the more professional tools, such as thermometers and scales, will serve you well in all your baking and cooking endeavors, making it worthwhile to invest in them.

Bowl and Mixing Spoon

If available, mixing can be done in an electric mixer with the mixer's flat beater, although a simple bowl and wooden spoon will easily do the job. For frosting, use whisk.

Cupcake and Muffin Pans

The most readily available pan is the standard 12 cup muffin pan, usually made from metal or Teflon. Silicon pans in various sizes and shapes, as well as pans with smaller cup circumference for mini cupcakes, are also available for purchase. Regardless of pan type, it is recommended to line the pans with cupcake or muffin liners before baking.

Measuring Tools

Baking is an exact science and there is significance to the proportions listed in a recipe, which is why I recommend working with measuring tools such as digital scales, measuring cups, teaspoons, tablespoons, a professional baking thermometer (home thermometers are not good substitutes...), etc. Such tools are available at specialty stores.

Oven

The type of oven used makes no difference, since ovens and their functions vary. Consequently, one must treat preparation times only as approximations, adjusting baking time and degrees according to the oven used.

Pastry Bags and Tip Sizes

Reusable pastry bags are available for purchase, as are disposable pastry bags that make filling and decorating cupcakes easier. Decorating tips come in various sizes and shapes allowing for a vast choice of designs.

Thin Sieve/Sifter

Professional sifters are available for purchase, but a regular dense sieve can be a simple and equally useful solution. It's important to understand that the purpose of sifting is to introduce air to the mixture, a function that makes it lighter, which is why one should not skip the sifting of dry ingredients.

Timer

As mentioned, exact timing is crucial in baking, making timers a necessary tool.

Wire Cooling Rack

Once baked, cupcakes must be cooled to prevent steam from collecting at the bottom of the pan, which will turn the base of the cupcakes damp and spongy.

Ingredients

~~~~~~

Butter
To achieve a rich tasting mixture, it is recommended to use unsalted, room-temperature butter.

Decorations and Colorful Candies
Nowadays, selection is so plentiful that the sky is the limit. You can be as creative as you wish, making use of fruit, colorful candy, chocolates of various sizes, and any other garnish that will put a smile on your face. Make sure that the garnish you select is edible and stored in a dry, dark place to prevent its color from fading.

Eggs
Eggs make the texture of the cupcake batter richer and help bind ingredients together. It is recommended to use fresh medium size eggs at room temperature.

Flour
Generally, all purpose white flour combined with baking powder is used, although it is possible to use cake flour which already contains self-rising ingredients. In this case, leave out the baking powder. I will also introduce recipes that offer healthier flour substitutes such as corn flour, rice flour, potato flour and whole wheat flour, which create a denser and heavier textured cupcake. Such substitutes offer not only variety, but a fantastic solution for guests or relatives who may be sensitive to glutens, or who keep kosher during the Jewish holiday of Passover.

Sugar
Most of the recipes in this book call for white sugar, although there are also recipes that call for brown sugar, which gives texture and color to the cupcake. You can substitute the sugar, or mix it with other sweeteners such as honey, maple syrup, molasses or date honey.

Food Coloring
Grocery stores carry a large selection of food coloring, among which are powders, pastes, pens, liquids and more. These days, natural food coloring, which I highly recommend, is also available. Be sure to note expiration dates and storage instructions.

Golden Syrup
Golden syrup is a form of inverted sugar syrup. It is produced in the sugar cane refining process or by treatment of a sugar solution with acid. Golden syrup is amber-colored and serves as a honey substitute.

Sugar Dough
Sugar dough is available for purchase in various colors or in white, to which food coloring may be added.

Serving and Storage Suggestions

~~~~~~

There are several ways to serve cupcakes; this book refers to some of the more popular ones. A personal cupcake may accompany the traditional tea break or be served as a personalized dessert for each guest at the end of a meal. Cupcakes may be used as centerpieces, and even take the place of flowers or candles. As for storage, it is best to eat cupcakes when they are fresh out of the oven and slightly cooled. Leftovers can be stored in an airtight container in the refrigerator for up to three days.

Basic Recipes

As in everything in life, when it comes to cupcakes, a solid foundation is necessary for success. In the first part of the book, I've collected basic and easy-to-prepare recipes that constitute the foundation of baking cupcakes. These recipes offer a number of easy suggestions for glazes, frostings, and ganache. They can be enhanced as your heart and imagination desires.

~~~~~~

Chocolate Ganache
~~~~~~~~~~~~~~~~~~~~

It is preferable to use high quality chocolate. It is possible to substitute dark chocolate with white or milk chocolate, according to preference.

~~~~~~

INGREDIENTS

⅞ cup heavy whipping cream

1 cup dark chocolate, coarsely chopped

PREPARATION

1. In a small saucepan, bring cream just to a boil, remove from heat and pour over chocolate.

2. Wait about 1 minute until chocolate melts, then, with a whisk, mix cream and chocolate in center of bowl until smooth ganache consistency is achieved.

Classic Chocolate Cupcakes
~~~~~~~~~~~~~~~~~~~

Makes

~ 12 ~

Cupcakes

If you still nostalgically recall the taste of your classroom birthday cupcakes, this is the recipe for you. Top with your favorite frosting, some sprinkles, or enjoy plain with a glass of milk.
~~~~~~~~~~~~~~~~~~~~~~~~~~~~~~~~~~~~~~~

INGREDIENTS

2½ cups white flour

1 tablespoon baking powder

¼ teaspoon salt

¼ teaspoon baking soda

2 tablespoons cocoa powder

¼ cup high quality bittersweet chocolate

½ cup butter, at room temperature

1 cup sugar

1 tablespoon vanilla extract

3 eggs

1½ cups buttermilk

PREPARATION

1. Preheat the oven to 325°F. Insert liners into medium cupcake pans.

2. In a bowl, sift flour, baking powder, salt, baking soda, and cocoa powder.

3. Melt chocolate in a bowl placed over a pot of hot water (double boiler) and mix until smooth.

4. Place butter and sugar in a mixing bowl, beating with the mixer's flat beater on medium speed. Add vanilla extract and melted chocolate (scraping sides of bowl as needed), until the batter is light and airy.

5. Reduce mixing speed to low, add eggs one at a time, mixing well.

6. Gradually add dry mixture (prepared in Step 2) and buttermilk, mix until incorporated into a smooth batter.

7. Fill the cupcake liners two-thirds full.

8. Bake for 20-25 minutes, or until springy to the touch and a toothpick inserted in the cupcake's center comes out clean.

9. Remove cupcakes from pan and cool on wire rack for 10 minutes.

Vanilla Cupcakes

~~~~~~~~~~~~~~~~~~~~~

Makes

~ *12* ~

Cupcakes

INGREDIENTS

3 cups white flour

1 tablespoon baking powder

¼ teaspoon salt

¼ teaspoon baking soda

½ cup butter, at room temperature

1 cup sugar

1 tablespoon vanilla extract

2 eggs

1½ cups buttermilk

It can be argued that the world is divided into two kinds of people: chocolate people and vanilla people. This recipe is dedicated to the latter – and it's also one of the simplest recipes for the ultimate classic cupcake.

~~~~~~~~~~~~~~~~~~~~~~~~~~~~~~~~~~~~~~

PREPARATION

1. Preheat the oven to 325°F. Insert liners into medium cupcake pans.

2. In a bowl, sift flour, baking powder, salt and baking soda.

3. In a separate bowl, place butter and sugar, whip with the mixer's flat beater on medium speed. Add the vanilla extract (scraping sides of bowl) until the batter is light and airy.

4. Reduce mixing speed to low, add eggs one at a time, mixing well.

5. Gradually add dry ingredients and buttermilk, mixing well until batter is smooth.

6. Fill the cupcake liners two-thirds full.

7. Bake for 20-25 minutes, or until cupcakes are springy to the touch and a toothpick inserted into the cupcake's center comes out clean.

Egg White Royal Frosting

Royal Frosting is a pure white frosting that dries to a smooth matte finish. Traditionally it has been used for wedding cakes, gingerbread houses and cookies. This is also a great icing for intricate piping of decorations.

INGREDIENTS

1 egg white

¾ cup, plus 1 tablespoon powdered sugar

1 teaspoon lemon juice

PREPARATION

1. In a bowl, beat egg white while gradually adding powdered sugar until glaze thickens and shines.

2. Add lemon juice and continue beating mixture until a uniform consistency is achieved.

Cream Cheese Frosting

In addition to being a bit lighter than a classic buttercream frosting, cream cheese frosting offers a tanginess that livens up your cupcake.

INGREDIENTS

½ cup butter at room temperature

¾ cup cream cheese

1 tablespoon vanilla extract

3 cups powdered sugar

PREPARATION

1. In a bowl, mix butter, cream cheese and vanilla extract on low speed for about 1 minute.

2. Gradually add powdered sugar and mix for about 2 more minutes until smooth.

Dairy-free Cupcakes
~~~~~~~~~~~~~~~~~~~~~

Makes
~ 10 ~
Cupcakes

INGREDIENTS

2½ cups white flour

1 tablespoon baking powder

¼ teaspoon salt

¼ tablespoon baking soda

3 eggs

1 cup sugar

1 tablespoon vanilla extract

⅔ cup canola oil

¼ cup water

This is a terrific recipe for people with dairy allergies or lactose intolerance. Not only is this recipe oh-so-simple, but it also allows you to cut out the butter while still enjoying a scrumptious cupcake!
~~~~~~~~~~~~~~~~~~~~~~~~~~~~~~~~~~~~~~~

PREPARATION

1. Preheat the oven to 325°F. Insert liners into medium cupcake pans.

2. In a bowl, sift flour, baking powder, salt and baking soda.

3. In a separate bowl, mix eggs, sugar and vanilla extract on medium speed.

4. Gradually add dry ingredients (prepared in Step 2), oil and water, mix until batter is smooth and uniform.

5. Fill lined cupcake pan two-thirds full.

6. Bake for 20-25 minutes, or until cupcakes are springy to the touch and a toothpick inserted in cupcake's center comes out clean.

Buttercream Frosting

~~~~~~~~~~~~~~~~~~~~~

This buttercream frosting recipe is actually an old-fashioned butter and powdered sugar frosting that is popular in America. Make sure to beat for the required time in order to achieve the creamy texture.

~~~~~~

INGREDIENTS

½ cup butter at room temperature

2 tablespoons milk

1 tablespoon vanilla extract

3 cups powdered sugar

PREPARATION

1. In a mixer, beat butter for 1 minute, gradually adding milk, vanilla extract, and powdered sugar.

2. Mix for 3 minutes until frosting is smooth and uniform.

Chocolate Buttercream Frosting

~~~~~~~~~~~~~~~~~~~~~

This recipe is a chocolate version of the classic rich butter frosting. Chocolate lovers can enjoy it on a classic chocolate cupcake, or mix and match with vanilla cupcakes for variety.

~~~~~~

INGREDIENTS

¾ cup butter at room temperature

4 level tablespoons cocoa powder

3 tablespoons boiling water

3 cups powdered sugar

PREPARATION

1. In mixer, beat butter.

2. In separate bowl, sift cocoa powder and add boiling water. Mix until paste is uniform.

3. Transfer paste to the mixing bowl containing the butter, gradually adding powdered sugar. Beat for about 1 minute to achieve smooth, uniform consistency.

Lemon Frosting
~~~~~~~~~~~~~~~~~~~

This lemon frosting recipe is a tart take on classic buttercream. Enjoy on vanilla cupcakes, or whichever cupcake would suit a lemon kick.
~~~~~~~~~~~~~~~~~~~~~~~~~~~~~~~~~~~~~~~

INGREDIENTS

Juice of 3 lemons

Zest of 3 lemons

1¼ cups sugar

3 eggs

4 egg yolks

⅔ cup butter at room temperature

PREPARATION

1. Pour lemon juice, lemon zest, sugar, eggs and yolks into a bowl placed over a pot of hot water (double boiler) stirring constantly until sugar is dissolved.

2. Add half the butter and continue stirring. At this point the eggs will begin to harden. Continue beating and add the remaining butter. It's important to continue stirring to avoid further hardening of the eggs.

3. Remove from heat and strain through dense sieve to remove hardened egg pieces and lemon zest.

Fondant Glaze
~~~~~~~~~~~~~~~~~~~

This recipe is for those especially devoted souls, since it demands time and expertise. Yet, it really is worth the effort. Of course, it is also possible to purchase ready made fondant glazing at specialty bakeries.
~~~~~~~~~~~~~~~~~~~~~~~~~~~~~~~~~~~~~~~

INGREDIENTS

1 cup water

2½ cups sugar

⅖ tablespoon gluten

A few drops of lemon juice

Thermometer

PREPARATION

1. In a pot, heat water and sugar, adding the gluten and bringing the temperature to 240-250°F (a thermometer is necessary).

2. Add lemon juice (it softens and improves texture).

3. Pour the batter into a mixing bowl and beat on slow speed for 40 minutes.

4. 15 minutes after mixing has begun, add a few drops of lemon juice, saving the remaining juice to add in the final few minutes of mixing.

Powdered Sugar and Lemon Glaze

INGREDIENTS

Juice of 3 lemons

½ cup water

2½ cups powdered sugar

When your cupcakes call out for delicate glaze instead of a thick frosting, this lemon glaze is perfect. The glaze can be made up to a day in advance – and stored at room temperature.

PREPARATION

1. Preheat the oven to 325°F.

2. In a small saucepan, heat lemon juice and water, then pour warm liquid into a bowl with the powdered sugar and stir.

3. Return entire mixture to pot and heat over low flame while stirring.

4. Pour over cupcakes and wait for about 5 minutes until cool.

5. Place in oven for 10-20 seconds (until bubbling, then immediately remove) for liquids to evaporate and glaze to harden.

Meringue Frosting

INGREDIENTS

8 egg whites

2½ cups sugar

½ tablespoon cream of tartar powder

Similar to Royal Frosting, meringue frosting is a lighter, fluffier version, perfect for placing little clouds atop your cupcakes.

PREPARATION

1. Pour all ingredients (egg whites, sugar, cream of tartar) into a bowl placed over a pot of hot water (double boiler), whisking constantly for 5 minutes or until mixture melts and is hot to the touch.

2. Transfer to mixing bowl and beat on medium speed, then high until mixture cools completely and the meringue is set.

The Classics, Cupcake Style
~~~~~~

Ginger Orange Cupcakes

Maple-Pecan Cupcakes

Strawberry Shortcake Cupcakes

Apple-Cinnamon Cupcakes

Gingerbread Cupcakes

Pear Crumble Cupcakes

Black Forest Cupcakes

Chocolate Mint Cupcakes

Lemon Cupcakes

Chocolate Chip Cupcakes

Honey Cupcakes for Winnie the Pooh

Banana Chocolate Cupcakes

Blueberry Cupcakes with Vanilla Cream

Coconut Cupcakes

Marble Cupcakes

New York Cheese Cupcakes

Ginger Orange Cupcakes
~~~~~~~~~~~~~~~~~~~~~

Makes

~ 12 ~

Cupcakes

INGREDIENTS

3 cups white flour

1 tablespoon baking powder

¼ teaspoon salt

¼ teaspoon baking soda

½ cup butter, at room temperature

1¼ cups sugar

3 eggs

½ cup orange juice

1 tablespoon fresh, thinly grated ginger

Garnish:

Tangerine or mandarin wedges

Glaze:

2 tablespoons orange juice

2 tablespoons lemon juice

1 cup powdered sugar

The combination of the warm and fragrant flavors of ginger and orange always lifts my spirits. The tanginess of the orange combines beautifully with hints of ginger to create an unexpected cupcake.

~~~~~~

PREPARATION

1. Preheat the oven to 325°F. Insert liners into medium cupcake pans.

2. Prepare cupcakes: In a bowl, sift flour, baking powder, salt and baking soda.

3. Place butter and sugar in a mixing bowl, beating with the mixer's flat beater at medium speed until mixture is light and airy.

4. Reduce mixing speed to low, add eggs one at a time, mixing well. Add half the orange juice and the ginger to the batter.

5. Gradually add half the amount of the dry ingredients (prepared in Step 2), mixing until incorporated. Add remaining half of orange juice and remaining half of dry ingredients, mixing until batter is smooth.

6. Fill the cupcake liners two-thirds full. Bake for 20-25 minutes, or until cupcakes are springy to the touch and a toothpick inserted in cupcake's center comes out clean.

7. Remove from oven and cool on wire rack for 10 minutes.

8. Prepare garnish: Using a sharp and flexible knife, slice unpeeled tangerine/mandarin to expose top and bottom of fruit. Continue to slice around the body of the fruit, through the peel and beyond the pith covering the fruit, exposing the wedges.

9. Insert knife diagonally into the inner part of each wedge attached to the pith, then again on the other side until you have a clean section, without pith.

10. Prepare glaze: Pour orange juice, lemon juice and powdered sugar into a small saucepan on low heat, mixing for about 2 minutes until liquids slightly evaporate.

11. Remove from heat and glaze cupcakes with a tablespoon each. Wait about 5 minutes for glaze to cool and harden before topping with a tangerine wedge (prepared in Steps 8 and 9) for garnish.

Maple-Pecan Cupcakes

~~~~~~~~~~~~~~~~~~~

Makes

~ *12* ~

Cupcakes

INGREDIENTS

3 cups white flour

¼ teaspoon salt

1 tablespoon baking powder

¼ teaspoon baking soda

½ cup butter, at room temperature

1 cup maple syrup

2 eggs

2 cups milk

¾ cup chopped pecans

Frosting:

1 cup heavy whipping cream

½ cup maple syrup

½ cup chopped candied pecans

Maple syrup is a sweetener produced from the sap of the maple tree. Although often relegated to a topper for pancakes, waffles or French toast, maple syrup stars as the main attraction in this recipe, revealing itself as a mouth-watering alternative to standard sugar.

~~~~~~~~~~~~~~~~~~~~~~~~~~~~~~~~~~~~~~~

PREPARATION

1. Preheat the oven to 325°F. Insert liners into medium cupcake pans.

2. Prepare cupcakes: In a bowl, sift flour, salt, baking powder and baking soda.

3. In a mixing bowl, beat butter with the mixer's flat beater on medium speed.

4. Add maple syrup to butter and continue beating until mixture is light and airy.

5. Reduce mixing speed to low, add eggs one at a time, mixing well.

6. Gradually add dry ingredients (prepared in Step 2) and milk, mix until well incorporated into smooth batter.

7. Mix in chopped pecans by hand.

8. Fill the cupcake liners two-thirds full.

9. Bake for 20-25 minutes, or until cupcakes are springy to the touch and a toothpick inserted into the cupcake's center comes out clean.

10. Remove from oven and cool on wire rack for 10 minutes.

11. Prepare frosting: In a bowl, whip cream with 3 tablespoons maple syrup until firm frosting is achieved.

12. Fold chopped pecans into frosting.

13. Place dollop of maple frosting on each cupcake, adding a teaspoon of maple syrup on top of the frosting.

Strawberry Shortcake Cupcakes
~~~~~~~~~~~~~~~~~~~~~

Makes

~ *12* ~

Cupcakes

INGREDIENTS

2 cups white flour

¼ teaspoon salt

1 tablespoon baking soda

4 eggs

1 tablespoon vanilla extract

1½ cups sugar

½ cup whole milk

Filling and frosting:

3 cups fresh, washed strawberries, sliced into 1" cubes, without stems

⅓ cup sugar

1 tablespoon pure vanilla extract

2 tablespoons balsamic vinegar

2 cups whipping cream

¼ cup powdered sugar

12 small, whole strawberries, washed and dried, with stems intact

I adapted this well-known and classic strawberry shortcake recipe to the measurements of a cupcake, with a surprising addition – balsamic vinegar. The combination of the balsamic vinegar and strawberry shortcake (both of Italian origins) improves upon an old favorite, giving it an enjoyable and unexpected kick.
~~~~~~~~~~~~~~~~~~~~~~~~~~~~~~~~~~~~~~~

PREPARATION

1. Preheat the oven to 325°F. Insert liners into medium cupcake pans.

2. Prepare cupcakes: In a bowl, sift flour, salt and baking soda. On medium speed, beat eggs, vanilla extract, and sugar for about 3 minutes or until mixture is light and airy.

3. Reduce mixing speed to low and gradually add dry ingredients (prepared in Step 2). Slowly add milk, until a smooth batter is achieved. Scrape sides of bowl as needed. Fill the cupcake liners two-thirds full.

4. Bake for 20-25 minutes, or until cupcakes are springy to the touch and a toothpick inserted in the cupcake's center comes out clean. Remove from oven and cool on wire rack for 10 minutes.

5. Prepare filling and frosting: Place sliced strawberries in a bowl with sugar, vanilla extract and 1 tablespoon of balsamic vinegar, mix. It is recommended to let the mixture rest for about 20 minutes so the flavors can incorporate.

6. Carefully remove cupcake liners, and with the help of a serrated knife, slice cupcakes horizontally into three equal layers.

7. In a mixing bowl, beat whipping cream with powdered sugar and vanilla extract until cream is set, but still soft.

8. Assemble: start with bottom layer of cupcake, pour 1 heaping tablespoon of cream, topped with 1 tablespoon of sliced strawberries and a bit of their liquid. Next, top with second cake layer, pressing down gently, repeat for third layer. On top layer of cake, place a tablespoon of cream in center, leaving perimeters bare. Top center with whole strawberry with stem. Serve immediately.

Apple-Cinnamon Cupcakes
~~~~~~~~~~~~~~~~~~

Makes
~ *12* ~
Cupcakes

INGREDIENTS

2 cups white flour

1 cup whole wheat flour

1 tablespoon baking powder

¼ teaspoon salt

¼ teaspoon baking soda

1½ tablespoons ground cinnamon

½ cup butter, at room temperature

⅓ cup sugar

2 eggs

1½ cups sweetened apple cider

2 apples, halved and thinly sliced

½ cup cinnamon sugar

This winning combination is comfort food at its best. I love using red apples that blend well with the woody scent of cinnamon.
~~~~~~~~~~~~~~~~~~~~~~~~~~~~~~~~~~~

PREPARATION

1. Preheat the oven to 325°F. Insert liners into medium cupcake pans.

2. Prepare cupcakes: In a bowl, sift white flour, whole wheat flour, baking powder, salt, baking soda, and cinnamon.

3. Place butter and sugar in a mixing bowl, beat with the mixer's flat beater on medium speed until mixture is light and airy.

4. Reduce mixing speed to low, add eggs one at a time, mixing well.

5. Gradually add dry ingredients (prepared in Step 2), and cider, mixing well until batter is smooth.

6. Fill the cupcake liners two-thirds full.

7. Top cupcake batter with apple slices, fan-like, with each slice partially dipped into the batter.

8. Bake for 20-25 minutes, until cupcakes are springy to the touch and a toothpick inserted in cupcake's center comes out clean.

9. Remove from oven and cool on wire rack for 10 minutes.

10. Decorate: Before serving, sprinkle cupcakes with cinnamon sugar.

Gingerbread
Cupcakes
~~~~~~~~~~~~~~~~~~~

Makes

~ *12* ~

Cupcakes

INGREDIENTS

2½ cups white flour

¼ teaspoon salt

1 tablespoon baking powder

½ tablespoon ground ginger

¼ tablespoon ground nutmeg

½ tablespoon ground cinnamon

¼ teaspoon baking soda

½ cup butter, at room temperature

1 cup brown sugar

2 tablespoons golden syrup

2 eggs

½ cup whole milk

These sticky, spicy brown cakes are as good as it gets. If you'd like to top them, I recommend a simple powdered sugar and lemon glaze (see page 19) so as not to overpower the various spices in the cupcakes.

~~~~~~

PREPARATION

1. Preheat the oven to 325°F. Insert liners into medium cupcake pans.

2. In a bowl, sift flour, salt, baking powder, ginger, cinnamon, nutmeg, and baking soda.

3. Place butter and sugar in a mixing bowl, beating on medium speed.

4. Add golden syrup and mix until a light and airy batter is achieved (scraping sides of bowl as needed).

5. Reduce mixing speed to low, add eggs one at a time, mixing well.

6. Add small amounts of the dry ingredients (prepared in Step 2), alternating with small amounts of milk until mixture is completely integrated and smooth.

7. Fill the cupcake liners two-thirds full.

8. Bake for 20-25 minutes, or until cupcakes are springy to the touch and a toothpick inserted in cupcake's center comes out clean.

9. Remove from oven and cool on a wire rack for 10 minutes.

Pear Crumble Cupcakes
~~~~~~~~~~~~~~~~~~~~

Makes
~ *42* ~
Mini Cupcakes

INGREDIENTS

Pear cubes:

4 pears

1 cup water

1 cup sugar

1 cinnamon stick

Cupcakes:

3 cups white flour

1 tablespoon baking powder

¼ teaspoon salt

¼ teaspoon baking soda

½ cup butter, at room temperature

1 cup sugar

1 tablespoon vanilla extract

2 eggs

1 cup milk

This is a more interesting take on the traditional apple crumble. The pear cubes lend the cupcakes moistness and a melt-in-your-mouth texture which juxtapose the crunchiness of the pastry crumbs, creating a textural celebration. Try to serve warm with a side of vanilla ice cream.

~~~~~~~~~~~~~~~~~~~~~~~~~~~~~~~~~~~~~~~

PREPARATION

1. Preheat the oven to 325°F. Insert liners into mini cupcake pans.

2. Prepare pear cubes: Peel pears and remove seeds with a spoon, cut into 1" cubes.

3. In a small saucepan bring water and sugar to a boil, along with the cinnamon stick, to create sugar syrup.

4. Once the sugar has dissolved, add pear cubes and cook for another 5 minutes until partially soft. It's important that the pears not be too soft since they will be further baked.

5. Remove from heat, drain syrup and cool completely. You may want to reserve the syrup and use it as a substitute for maple syrup on pancakes, toast or as a sweetener on fruit salad, etc.

6. Prepare cupcakes: In a bowl, sift flour, baking powder, salt and baking soda.

7. Place butter and sugar in a mixing bowl, beating with the mixer's flat beater on medium speed. Add vanilla extract (scraping sides of bowl as needed), until a light and airy mixture is achieved.

8. Reduce mixing speed to low, add eggs one at a time, mixing well.

9. Gradually add dry ingredients (prepared in Step 6) and milk, mixing until batter is smooth.

10. Add pear cubes to batter, mix in by hand.

(continued on page 30)

(continued from page 28)

Topping:

½ cup white sugar

½ cup brown sugar

¼ teaspoon salt

2 teaspoons cinnamon

1 cup white flour

¾ cup cold cubed butter

Frosting:

¾ cup butter, at room temperature

3¾ cups powdered sugar

3 tablespoons mascarpone cheese

2 tablespoons of the sugar in which the pears were cooked

11. Fill the cupcake liners two-thirds full.

12. Bake for 20-25 minutes, or until cupcakes are springy to the touch and a toothpick inserted in cupcake's center comes out clean.

13. Remove from oven and cool on wire rack for 10 minutes.

14. Prepare topping: In a bowl, mix white sugar, brown sugar, salt and cinnamon.

15. Add flour and cold butter cubes, mixing on low speed until coarse crumbs are created. These crumbs can also be made by hand: roll butter between fingers until small crumbs are made, no larger than ¼". Place dough crumbs in a covered bowl and refrigerate for 1 hour.

16. After refrigeration, pre-heat oven to 325°F. Scatter crumbs on a lined baking sheet and bake for about 8 minutes until golden brown.

17. Prepare frosting: Beat butter with powdered sugar, mascarpone cheese, and sugar until smooth.

18. Place one tablespoon of frosting on each cupcake, sprinkling baked topping on each.

Black Forest Cupcakes

~~~~~~~~~~~~~~~~~~~

Makes

~ *12* ~

Cupcakes

INGREDIENTS

6 tablespoons coarsely chopped bittersweet chocolate

2 cups white flour

¼ teaspoon salt

1 tablespoon baking powder

1 tablespoon cocoa

¼ teaspoon baking soda

½ cup butter, at room temperature

1 cup sugar

5 tablespoons kirsch liqueur

2 eggs

3 tablespoons pitted, maraschino cherries

Frosting:

½ cup + ⅔ cup whipping cream

½ cup chopped dark chocolate

2 tablespoons kirsch liqueur

2 tablespoons powdered sugar

12 maraschino cherries

This cupcake is inspired by the classic Black Forest cake, a rich decadent cake filled with maraschino cherries, kirsch liqueur and glazed with a rich chocolate ganache. To make this cupcake all the more sinful, a dollop of sweet cream and a cherry decorate the top.

~~~~~~

PREPARATION

1. Preheat the oven to 325°F. Insert liners into medium cupcake pans.

2. Prepare cupcakes: Melt dark chocolate in a bowl placed over a pot of hot water (double boiler).

3. In a bowl, sift flour, salt, baking powder, cocoa and baking soda.

4. Place butter and sugar in a mixing bowl, beat with the mixer's flat beater on medium speed. Add kirsch liqueur and mix until mixture is light and airy (scrape sides of bowl as needed).

5. Reduce mixing speed to low, add eggs one at a time, mixing well. Gradually add dry ingredients (prepared in Step 3) to the batter, adding the melted chocolate, mixing until all ingredients are incorporated into a smooth batter.

6. Add cherries to batter, mixing by hand. Fill the cupcake liners two-thirds full.

7. Bake for 20-25 minutes, or until cupcakes are springy to the touch and a toothpick inserted in cupcake's center comes out clean. Remove from oven and cool on wire rack for 10 minutes.

8. Prepare frosting: In a small saucepan, heat ½ cup whipping cream to boiling point, remove from heat and pour over chocolate.

9. Wait about 1 minute for chocolate to melt, then whisk cream and chocolate in the center of the bowl until a thick ganache cream is achieved, add the kirsch liqueur and mix.

10. Whip powdered sugar with ⅔ cup whipping cream until cream is smooth.

11. Spread a layer of chocolate ganache on top of each cupcake, followed by 1 tablespoon of whipped cream and a cherry.

Chocolate Mint Cupcakes
~~~~~~~~~~~~~~~~~~

Makes
~ *12* ~
Cupcakes

There is something a bit curious about the chocolate-mint flavor combination; yet somehow, this inexplicable combination works. In this elegant and simple to prepare recipe, I recommend using small fresh mint leaves for garnish, which adds both in refreshing flavor and presentation.
~~~~~~~~~~~~~~~~~~~~~~~~~~~~~~~~~~~~~~

INGREDIENTS

1 cup coarsely chopped bittersweet chocolate

2 tablespoons peppermint extract

2½ cups white flour

2 tablespoons baking powder

¼ teaspoon salt

¼ teaspoon baking soda

½ cup butter, at room temperature

1½ cups sugar

2 eggs

½ cup sour cream

Chocolate ganache:

1 cup + 2½ tablespoons coarsely chopped dark chocolate

¾ cup whipping cream

Garnish:

30 small mint leaves

½ cup mint flavored chocolate

PREPARATION

1. Preheat the oven to 325°F. Insert liners into medium cupcake pans.

2. Prepare cupcakes: Melt dark chocolate in a bowl placed over a pot of hot water (double boiler), add peppermint extract, remove from heat and cool slightly.

3. In a bowl, sift flour, baking powder, salt and baking soda.

4. Place butter and sugar in a mixing bowl, beating on medium speed until mixture is light and airy. Reduce mixing speed to low, add eggs one at a time, mixing well.

5. Add the melted chocolate to the prepared batter, mixing until texture is smooth and integrated. Gradually add dry ingredients (prepared in step 3) and sour cream, mixing well until batter is smooth.

6. Fill the cupcake liners two-thirds full. Bake for 20-25 minutes, or until cupcakes are springy and a toothpick inserted in cupcake's center comes out clean.

7. Remove from oven and cool on wire rack for 10 minutes.

8. Prepare chocolate ganache: With the help of a sharp knife, cut chocolate mint into shavings (tip – freezing the chocolate prevents it from melting and makes it easier to cut).

9. In a small saucepan, heat cream to boiling point, pouring it over the chopped dark chocolate, wait about 1 minute for chocolate to melt. Whisk together chocolate and cream in center of bowl until a thick ganache cream is achieved.

10. Cool for about 10 minutes. Place a tablespoon of ganache on each cupcake, sprinkle with chocolate shavings and mint leaves. It's best to add the fresh mint just before serving to prevent the leaves from browning or wilting.

Lemon Cupcakes

~~~~~~~~~~~~~~~~~~~

Makes

~ *12* ~

Cupcakes

INGREDIENTS

1 cup + 2 tablespoons butter

Zest of 3 lemons

2½ cups white flour

1 teaspoon baking powder

¼ teaspoon salt

3 eggs

1¼ cups sugar

Glaze:

½ cup butter, at room temperature

2½ cups powdered sugar

4 tablespoons lemon juice

Garnish:

Lemon zest, sugar crystal rose petals and sugar crystal violets

This is one of my favorite cupcakes. The tartness of the lemon juice lends it a refreshing and light quality, while the lemon zest gives it that extra special something which turns it into an especially pleasurable dessert.

~~~~~~~~~~~~~~~~~~~~~~~~~~~~~~~~~~~~~~

PREPARATION

1. Preheat the oven to 325°F. Insert liners into medium cupcake pans.

2. Prepare cupcakes: Melt butter and lemon zest on low heat; the heat helps release the flavors and spice the butter.

3. In a bowl, sift flour, baking powder and salt.

4. Place eggs and sugar in a mixing bowl, beating on medium speed.

5. Gradually add in the dry ingredients (prepared in Step 3), alternating with the melted butter (prepared in Step 2) and mix until mixture is light and airy.

6. Refrigerate batter for about 1 hour, until firm.

7. Fill the cupcake liners two-thirds full.

8. Bake for 20-25 minutes, or until cupcakes are springy to the touch and a toothpick inserted in cupcake's center comes out clean.

9. Remove from oven and cool on wire rack for 10 minutes.

10. Prepare glaze: In an electric mixer, beat butter with powdered sugar and lemon juice on low speed until frosting is integrated and smooth. (Add 1 more tablespoon of lemon juice for creamier texture if desired.)

11. Using a spatula, spread about ¼" of frosting on each cupcake, decorating with lemon zest and candied roses and violets.

Chocolate Chip Cupcakes
~~~~~~~~~~~~~~~~~~~~

Makes
~ *12* ~
Cupcakes

INGREDIENTS

2½ cups white flour

1 tablespoon baking powder

¼ teaspoon salt

¼ teaspoon baking soda

⅔ cup butter, at room temperature

1½ cups sugar

1 tablespoon vanilla extract

½ tablespoon almond extract

2 eggs

1 cup milk

½ cup dark chocolate chips

Frosting:

⅔ cup dark chocolate, coarsely chopped

3½ tablespoons butter, at room temperature

A pinch of salt

¾ cup sweetened condensed milk

1 heaping tablespoon light corn syrup

Traditional at its best, this basic old fashioned combination remains a favorite despite new and improved recipes. When I really crave something sweet, this recipe wins out every time.
~~~~~~

PREPARATION

1. Preheat the oven to 325°F. Insert liners into medium cupcake pans.

2. Prepare cupcakes: In a bowl, sift flour, baking powder, salt and baking soda.

3. Place butter, sugar, vanilla extract and almond extract in mixing bowl, beating on medium speed until mixture is light and airy.

4. Reduce speed to low, add eggs one at a time, mixing well.

5. Gradually add one third of the dry ingredients (prepared in Step 2), one third of the milk, and repeat 3 times. Mix until ingredients are incorporated and batter is smooth.

6. Add chocolate chips to mixture and stir.

7. Fill the cupcake liners two-thirds full.

8. Bake for 20-25 minutes, or until cupcakes are springy to the touch and a toothpick inserted in cupcake's center comes out clean.

9. Remove from oven and cool on wire rack for 10 minutes.

10. Prepare frosting: In a bowl placed over a pot of hot water (double boiler), melt chocolate and butter, mixing until texture is smooth.

11. Add salt, condensed milk, and corn syrup, mix.

12. Remove from heat and set aside to cool. When frosting cools and sets, spread a heaping tablespoon on top of each cupcake.

Honey Cupcakes for Winnie the Pooh
~~~~~~~~~~~~~~~~~~~

Makes

~ *12* ~

Cupcakes

INGREDIENTS

3 cups white flour

1 tablespoon baking powder

¼ teaspoon salt

¼ teaspoon clove

¼ teaspoon baking soda

⅔ cup butter, at room temperature

1 cup honey

1 tablespoon vanilla extract

2 eggs

1 prepared cup of chamomile tea

Frosting:

¾ cup butter, at room temperature

4 tablespoons mascarpone cheese

2 tablespoons honey

2 cups powdered sugar

Honey is credited with many qualities, with some people even claiming that honey is more beneficial than antibiotics. I tend to agree with Winnie the Pooh, who said "And the only reason for making honey is so as I can eat it."
(From A.A Milne's, Winnie the Pooh)
~~~~~~

PREPARATION

1. Preheat the oven to 325°F. Insert liners into medium cupcake pans.

2. Prepare cupcakes: Sift flour, baking powder, salt, clove, and baking soda into a bowl.

3. In a mixing bowl, cream butter with the mixer's flat beater at medium speed. Add honey and vanilla extract (scraping sides of bowl when needed), until mixture is light and airy.

4. Reduce mixing speed to low, add eggs one at a time, mixing well.

5. Gradually add dry ingredients (prepared in Step 2), alternating with tea, starting and ending with the flour mixture until all ingredients are incorporated into a smooth batter.

6. Fill the cupcake liners two-thirds full.

7. Bake for 20-25 minutes, or until cupcakes are springy to the touch and a toothpick inserted in cupcake's center comes out clean.

8. Remove from oven and cool on wire rack for 10 minutes.

9. Prepare frosting: With an electric mixer on low speed, mix butter, mascarpone, and honey for about 2 minutes until texture is creamy and smooth.

10. Gradually add powdered sugar, continuing to beat for 2-3 minutes until frosting is light and smooth.

11. Place a generous tablespoon of frosting on each cupcake.

Banana Chocolate Cupcakes
~~~~~~~~~~~~~~~~~~~

Makes

~ 12 ~

Cupcakes

INGREDIENTS

3 cups white flour

1 tablespoon baking powder

¼ teaspoon salt

¼ teaspoon nutmeg

½ cup butter, at room temperature

1¼ cups sugar

2 eggs

1 cup banana purée (ripe bananas mashed in food processor)

3½ tablespoons milk chocolate shavings

Frosting:

¾ cup + 1 tablespoon Philadelphia cream cheese

1 cup powdered sugar

2 tablespoons banana liqueur

Garnish:

⅔ cup milk chocolate shavings

1 thinly sliced banana

The delicate flavor of banana combines beautifully with milk chocolate shavings. I prefer to use small delicate shavings (as pictured), as opposed to chocolate chips which, once baked, tend to dominate the cupcake's delicate banana flavor.
~~~~~~~~~~~~~~~~~~~~~~~~~~~~~~~~~~~~

PREPARATION

1. Preheat the oven to 325°F. Insert liners into medium cupcake pans.

2. Prepare cupcakes: In a bowl, sift flour, baking powder, salt and nutmeg.

3. Place butter and sugar in mixing bowl, beating with the mixer's flat beater on medium speed until mixture is light and airy.

4. Reduce speed to low, add eggs one at a time, mixing well.

5. Add half the flour mixture (prepared in Step 2), banana purée and then remaining flour mixture.

6. Finally, add chocolate shavings and stir.

7. Fill the cupcake liners two-thirds full.

8. Bake for 20-25 minutes, or until cupcakes are springy to the touch and a toothpick inserted in cupcake's center comes out clean.

9. Remove from oven and cool on wire rack for 10 minutes.

10. Prepare frosting: In an electric mixer, beat cream cheese for about 2 minutes, until cheese is soft and smooth. Add powdered sugar and banana liqueur. Continue beating mixture until frosting is smooth.

11. With a spatula, spread frosting on each cooled cupcake, garnish with sliced bananas and chocolate shavings.

Blueberry Cupcakes with Vanilla Cream

~~~~~~~~~~~~~~~~~~~

Makes

~ 12 ~

Cupcakes

INGREDIENTS

3 cups white flour

1 tablespoon baking powder

¼ teaspoon salt

¼ teaspoon baking soda

½ cup butter, at room temperature

1 cup sugar

4 eggs

1⅔ cups fresh blueberries

Frosting:

3 egg yolks

½ cup sugar

2 tablespoons vanilla extract

¼ cup white flour

3 tablespoons corn flour

1¼ cups milk

½ cup + 2½ tablespoons cubed butter, at room temperature

Garnish:

⅔ cup fresh blueberries

Blueberries have always been one of my favorite fruits – just as they are, as well as in this great recipe that flawlessly combines them with vanilla cream. It's always best to use fresh blueberries.

~~~~~~~~~~~~~~~~~~~~~~~~~~~~~~~~~~~~~~~

PREPARATION

1. Preheat the oven to 325°F. Insert liners into medium cupcake pans.

2. Prepare cupcakes: In a bowl, sift flour, baking powder, salt, and baking soda.

3. Place butter and sugar in mixing bowl, beating with the mixer's flat beater at medium speed until mixture is light and airy.

4. Reduce mixing speed to low, add eggs one at a time, mixing well. Gradually add dry ingredients (prepared in Step 2), mixing until incorporated into smooth batter.

5. Add blueberries and mix by hand. Fill the cupcake liners two-thirds full.

6. Bake for 20-25 minutes, or until cupcakes are springy to the touch and a toothpick inserted into cupcake's center comes out clean. Remove from oven and cool on wire rack for 10 minutes.

7. Prepare frosting: Beat egg yolks, sugar and vanilla extract, add flour and corn flour, mix. In a small saucepan, heat milk to boiling point. Transfer half of hot milk to egg mixture, then add remaining milk.

8. Return to saucepan over low heat, mix constantly for about 2-3 minutes until cream is thick. Remove from heat. Add half of butter and mix.

9. Transfer cream to a bowl to cool, placing wax paper directly on mixture to prevent skin from forming. Leave out (do not refrigerate) for complete cooling.

10. When cream has completely cooled, beat in remaining softened butter to create smooth cream.

11. Place a heaping tablespoon of cream on each cupcake, sprinkling a few fresh blueberries on top.

Coconut Cupcakes

~~~~~~~~~~~~~~~~~~~

Makes

~ 12 ~

mini cupcakes

INGREDIENTS

3 cups white flour

1 tablespoon baking powder

¼ teaspoon salt

¼ teaspoon baking soda

½ cup butter, at room temperature

1 cup sugar

1 tablespoon vanilla extract

2 eggs

1 cup coconut milk

½ cup shredded coconut

Frosting:

½ cup butter, at room temperature

¾ cup cream cheese

3 teaspoons coconut cream

1½ tablespoons powdered sugar

Garnish:

1½ cups sweetened shredded coconut

This is an especially attractive and impressive cupcake. It's important to use large coconut flakes for the topping. If available, using semi-dry coconut shreds to guarantee the desired dramatic effect. This is a cupcake that tastes as good as it looks.

~~~~~~~~~~~~~~~~~~~~~~~~~~~~~~~~~~~~~~

PREPARATION

1. Preheat the oven to 325°F. Insert liners into medium cupcake pans.

2. Prepare cupcakes: In a bowl, sift flour, baking powder, salt, and baking soda.

3. Place butter, sugar, and vanilla extract in a mixing bowl, beating with the mixer's flat beater on medium speed until a light and airy mixture is achieved.

4. Reduce mixing speed to low, add eggs one at a time, mixing well.

5. Gradually add dry ingredients (prepared in Step 2), coconut milk, and shredded coconut, mixing until all ingredients are incorporated into a smooth batter.

6. Fill the cupcake liners two-thirds full.

7. Bake for 20-25 minutes, or until cupcakes are springy to the touch and a toothpick inserted in cupcake's center comes out clean.

8. Remove from oven and cool on wire rack for 10 minutes.

9. Prepare frosting: Using an electric mixer, blend butter, cream cheese and coconut cream on low speed for about 1 minute.

10. Gradually add powdered sugar and continue mixing for about 2 more minutes until frosting is smooth and integrated.

11. Spread frosting on top of each cupcake, sprinkling generously with shredded coconut.

Marble Cupcakes

~~~~~~~~~~~~~~~~~~~

Makes
~ 12 ~
Cupcakes

INGREDIENTS

3½ tablespoons dark chocolate

¼ cup milk

1 tablespoon cocoa

3 cups white flour

2 tablespoons baking powder

¼ teaspoon salt

¼ teaspoon baking soda

1 cup + 2 tablespoons butter, at room temperature

1¼ cups sugar

3 eggs

1 tablespoon vanilla extract

Frosting:

3½ tablespoons dark chocolate

4 tablespoons milk

¾ cup + 2 tablespoons Philadelphia cream cheese

1 cup unsalted butter, at room temperature

4 cups powdered sugar

The best of both worlds, marble brings the unique flavors of chocolate and vanilla together in a single cake. When preparing these cupcakes, be sure to loosely swirl the two batters so that each bite will contain both chocolate and vanilla.

~~~~~~

PREPARATION

1. Preheat the oven to 325°F. Insert liners into medium cupcake pans.

2. Prepare cupcakes: Melt dark chocolate with 2 tablespoons milk in a bowl placed over a pot of hot water (double boiler). Once melted add cocoa and mix. Remove from heat and cool slightly.

3. In a bowl, sift flour, baking powder, salt, and baking soda.

4. Place butter and sugar in a mixing bowl, creaming with the mixer's flat beater on medium speed to achieve a light and airy mixture. Reduce mixing speed to low, add eggs one at a time, mixing well.

5. Gradually add dry ingredients (prepared in Step 3) and milk, mixing until incorporated into a smooth batter. Divide batter into two bowls, adding melted chocolate into one of the bowls and mixing well. Add vanilla extract into the second bowl and mix well.

6. Fill the cupcake liners two-thirds full in the following way: Pour 1 tablespoon of the white batter into bottom of tins, then pour 1 tablespoon of chocolate batter on top. With a knife or toothpick, loosely swirl from the center (don't over-swirl).

7. Bake for 20-25 minutes, or until cupcakes are springy to the touch and a toothpick inserted into cupcake's center comes out clean.

8. Prepare frosting: Melt dark chocolate with milk in a bowl placed over a pot of hot water (double boiler). With an electric mixer on low speed, beat cream cheese and butter for 2 minutes.

9. Gradually add the powdered sugar while continuing to beat for another 2-3 minutes, until frosting is light and airy. Divide frosting into two bowls, add melted chocolate to one and mix well. Place 1 tablespoon of vanilla frosting on top of each cupcake, then add 1 tablespoon of chocolate frosting on top, swirling together gently with a toothpick.

New York Cheese Cupcakes
~~~~~~~~~~~~~~~~~~~~~

Makes
~ 12 ~
Cupcakes

This recipe is for an infamously rich cake, here further improved with white chocolate. Disguised as a cupcake when baked in individual cupcake tins, this is really more a cup of cheesecake. Labels aside, you'll be happy to adopt this recipe.
~~~~~~

INGREDIENTS

¾ cup + 2 tablespoons graham crackers, finely crushed

3⅓ tablespoons powdered sugar

½ cup melted butter

Filling:

2¼ cups soft cream cheese

½ cup sugar

3 eggs

1⅓ cups chopped white chocolate

½ cup whipping cream

1 tablespoon corn flour

Topping:

¾ cup sour cream

Garnish:

Blueberries

PREPARATION

1. Preheat the oven to 275°F. Insert liners into medium cupcake pans.

2. Prepare crust: Mix graham cracker crumbs with powdered sugar and butter, tightly packing a full tablespoon of the mixture into the bottom of each cupcake tin. Freeze for 10 minutes.

3. Prepare filling: In a bowl, mix cream cheese, sugar and eggs into a smooth mixture.

4. In a small saucepan, melt white chocolate and whipping cream, gradually adding corn flour.

5. Beat melted chocolate mixture (prepared in Step 4) with the cream cheese mixture (prepared in Step 3) until smooth.

6. Carefully pour the batter over graham cracker crust, filling each tin three-quarters full (leave room for topping).

7. Bake for 18 minutes, until cupcakes are firm at sides and nearly set in center.

8. Remove from oven, cool. Once cupcakes are cool, keep refrigerated.

9. Prepare topping: Beat sour cream until smooth, place one tablespoon in center of each cupcake.

10. Garnish with fresh blueberries.

Cupcakes for Kiddies

~~~~~~

Strawberry Surprise Cupcakes with
Strawberry Sorbet

Oreo Cupcakes

Craft Project Cupcakes

Caramel Sundae Cupcakes

Triple Chocolate Knockout Cupcakes

Lollipop Cupcakes

Peanut Butter and Jelly Cupcakes

Chocolate Mousse Madness Cupcakes

Mini-Me Marshmallow Cupcakes

Toffee Square Cupcake Surprise

Strawberry Surprise Cupcakes with Strawberry Sorbet

~~~~~~~~~~~~~~~~~~

Makes

~ *12* ~

Cupcakes

INGREDIENTS

3 cups white flour

1 tablespoon baking powder

¼ teaspoon salt

¼ teaspoon baking soda

½ cup butter, at room temperature

1 tablespoon rum extract

⅓ cup sugar

2 eggs

1½ cups buttermilk

¾ cup high quality strawberry preserves

Frosting:

2¼ cups high quality strawberry sorbet

I chose to use strawberry preserves for this recipe since I love biting into chunks of the fruit. For those who prefer a smoother texture, using strawberry jam (in which the fruit is already mashed) or working preserves through a sieve are equally tasty alternatives.

~~~~~~

PREPARATION

1. Preheat the oven to 325°F. Insert liners into medium cupcake pans.

2. In a bowl, sift flour, baking powder, salt and baking soda.

3. Cream butter, rum extract, and sugar in an electric mixer with the mixer's flat beater on medium speed, until mixture is light and airy.

4. Reduce mixing speed to low, add eggs one at a time, mixing well.

5. Gradually add dry ingredients (prepared in Step 2) and buttermilk, mix until batter is smooth.

6. Add strawberry preserves, mixing well.

7. Fill cupcake liners two-thirds full.

8. Bake for 20-25 minutes, or until cupcakes are springy to the touch and a toothpick inserted in cupcake's center comes out clean.

9. Remove from oven and cool on wire rack for 10 minutes.

10. Place a heaping tablespoon of strawberry sorbet on top of each cupcake immediately before serving.

Oreo Cupcakes

~~~~~~~~~~~~~~~~~~~~

Makes

~ *12* ~

Cupcakes

This is a winning combination for children and adults alike. The crushed cookies in the batter and frosting make this cupcake a crispy, crunchy mouthful.

~~~~~~

INGREDIENTS

2½ cups white flour

1 tablespoon baking powder

¼ teaspoon salt

¼ teaspoon baking soda

1 cup butter, at room temperature

1¼ cups sugar

4 eggs

8 finely chopped Oreo cookies

Frosting:

1 cup whipping cream

3 tablespoons powdered sugar

10 coarsely crushed Oreo cookies

PREPARATION

1. Preheat the oven to 325°F. Insert liners into medium cupcake pans.

2. Prepare cupcakes: In a bowl, sift flour, baking powder, salt and baking soda.

3. Cream butter and sugar in an electric mixer with the mixer's flat beater on medium speed until mixture is light and airy.

4. Reduce mixing speed to low, add eggs one at a time, mixing well.

5. Gradually add dry ingredients (prepared in Step 2) and the chopped Oreos, mixing until batter is smooth.

6. Fill the cupcake liners two-thirds full.

7. Bake for 20-25 minutes, or until cupcakes are springy to the touch and a toothpick inserted in cupcake's center comes out clean.

8. Remove from oven and cool on wire rack for 10 minutes.

9. Prepare frosting: With an electric mixer, beat whipping cream and powdered sugar until soft and creamy.

10. Add coarsely crushed Oreo pieces, gently mixing to prevent cookie pieces from breaking further.

11. Place a heaping tablespoon of frosting on top of each cupcake.

Craft Project Cupcakes

~~~~~~~~~~~~~~~~~~~~~

Makes

~ *12* ~

Cupcakes

INGREDIENTS

3 cups white flour

1 tablespoon baking powder

¼ teaspoon salt

½ cup butter, at room temperature

1 cup sugar

2 eggs

2 tablespoons vanilla extract

1½ cups buttermilk

Frosting:

¾ cup butter, at room temperature

3¾ cups powdered sugar

3 tablespoons mascarpone cheese

Red, yellow, green and blue food coloring

Multicolored M & M's

Multicolored candy sprinkles, sugar crystals

This type of do-it-yourself baking project is always an outrageous hit among children, especially at birthday parties. I recommend preparing the ingredients for frosting and candy toppings ahead of time and setting them out in pretty bowls. Then encourage your little guests to let their imaginations run wild.

~~~~~~

PREPARATION

1. Preheat the oven to 325°F. Insert liners into medium cupcake pans.

2. Prepare cupcakes: In a bowl, sift flour, baking powder and salt.

3. Cream butter and sugar in electric mixer with the mixer's flat beater on medium speed until mixture is light and airy.

4. Reduce mixing speed to low, add eggs one at a time, add vanilla extract, mixing well.

5. Gradually add dry ingredients (prepared in Step 2) and buttermilk, mixing until incorporated into a smooth batter.

6. Fill the cupcake liners two-thirds full.

7. Bake for 20-25 minutes, or until cupcakes are springy to the touch and a toothpick inserted in cupcake's center comes out clean.

8. Remove from oven, cool on wire rack for 10 minutes.

9. Prepare frosting: Cream butter with powdered sugar and mascarpone cheese until frosting is smooth.

10. Divide the frosting into 4 separate bowls, adding a few drops of food coloring to each and mixing. When using food coloring, it's preferable to start with just a few drops, mix and see the achieved color. More can always be added as desired.

11. Arrange the cupcakes, bowls of frosting and small bowls of candies on a tray in the middle of a table with tablespoons and spatulas. Allow children and other guests to create their personal cupcakes according to inspiration.

Caramel Sundae Cupcakes
~~~~~~~~~~~~~~~~~~~~

Makes
~ *12* ~
Cupcakes

For this recipe, I tried to combine cupcakes with my favorite ice cream sundae flavor – caramel. The combination produced a nutty tasting cupcake, topped with vanilla ice cream (invest in quality ice cream) and a rich caramel sauce sprinkled with peanuts. Of course you can always go crazy and add whipped cream, or substitute the caramel for chocolate syrup. When it comes to sundaes, anything goes!
~~~~~~

INGREDIENTS

3 cups white flour

1 tablespoon baking powder

¼ teaspoon salt

½ cup butter, at room temperature

¾ cup sugar

2 eggs

1 cup whole milk

3 tablespoons hazelnut spread

Caramel sauce:

1 teaspoon vanilla extract

1½ tablespoons butter, at room temperature

1 cup whipping cream

´ cup demerara sugar

1 tablespoon maple syrup

Garnish:

High quality vanilla ice cream

¼ cup roasted, unsalted peanuts

PREPARATION

1. Preheat the oven to 325°F. Insert liners into medium cupcake pans.

2. Prepare cupcakes: In a bowl, sift flour, baking powder and salt.

3. Cream butter and sugar in electric mixer with the mixer's flat beater on medium speed until mixture is light and airy.

4. Reduce mixing speed to low, add eggs one at a time, mixing well.

5. Gradually add dry ingredients (prepared in Step 2), milk and hazelnut spread, mix well until batter is smooth. Fill the cupcake liners two-thirds full.

6. Bake for 20-25 minutes, or until cupcakes are springy to the touch and a toothpick inserted in cupcake's center comes out clean.

7. Remove from oven and cool on wire rack for 10 minutes.

8. With the help of a serrated knife and a teaspoon, slice into the top of each cupcake, scooping out a small space for ice cream.

9. Prepare caramel sauce: In a small saucepan, heat vanilla extract, butter, and whipping cream.

10. In a pot, melt sugar and maple syrup until clear caramel is achieved.

11. Carefully add warmed cream mixture to caramel while mixing with a wooden spoon. Remove from heat and cool. Mixture can be refrigerated in a sealed container.

12. Place one scoop of vanilla ice cream in the space on top of each cupcake, drizzle caramel syrup on top, sprinkle on peanuts.

Triple Chocolate Knockout Cupcakes

Makes

~ 30 ~

Mini cupcakes

INGREDIENTS

⅔ cup coarsely chopped quality dark chocolate

2 tablespoons whipping cream

2 cups white flour

1 tablespoon baking powder

1 tablespoon cocoa powder

¼ teaspoon salt

½ cup butter, at room temperature

¾ cup sugar

2 eggs

½ cup white chocolate chips

⅓ cup dark chocolate chips

⅓ cup milk chocolate chips

This chocolate cupcake is so rich in chocolate that no frosting is needed. The combination of the three types of chocolate (dark, milk and white) is so decadent that you may want to save this recipe for special occasions, or bake the cupcakes as a gift for those truly addicted to chocolate.

PREPARATION

1. Preheat the oven to 325°F. Insert liners into mini cupcake pans.

2. In a bowl placed over a pot of hot water (double boiler), melt dark chocolate, adding whipping cream while constantly stirring until completely melted. Remove from heat and cool slightly.

3. In separate bowl, sift flour, baking powder, cocoa powder and salt.

4. Cream butter and sugar in electric mixer with the mixer's flat beater on medium speed until mixture is light and airy.

5. Reduce mixing speed to low, add eggs one at a time, mixing well.

6. Gradually add dry ingredients (prepared in Step 3) and melted chocolate until incorporated into a smooth batter.

7. Add all three types of chocolate chips, stir.

8. Fill the cupcake liners two-thirds full.

9. Bake for 10-12 minutes, or until cupcakes are springy to the touch and a toothpick inserted in cupcake's center comes out clean.

10. Remove from oven, cool on wire rack for 10 minutes.

Lollipop Cupcakes

~~~~~~~~~~~~~~~~~~~~

Makes

~ *20* ~

Mini vanilla cupcakes

INGREDIENTS

1 cup white flour

½ teaspoon baking powder

¼ teaspoon baking soda

¼ teaspoon salt

1 tablespoon vanilla extract

⅓ cup butter, at room temperature

½ cup sugar

1 egg

½ cup buttermilk

Makes

~ *20* ~

Mini chocolate cupcakes

INGREDIENTS

1 cup white flour

½ teaspoon baking powder

¼ teaspoon baking soda

¼ teaspoon salt

3 tablespoons quality cocoa powder

⅓ cup butter, at room temperature

½ cup sugar

1 egg

½ cup buttermilk

Accessories for assembly:

Cellophane paper

40 lollipop sticks

Satin ribbons

These cupcakes can be served at birthday parties as treats or prizes. In my experience, they are always a hit due to their minute size and unique presentation.

~~~~~~~~~~~~~~~~~~~~~~~~~~~~~~~~~~~~~~~

Preparation (Chocolate and Vanilla)

1. Preheat the oven to 325°F. Insert liners into mini cupcake pans.

2. Prepare cupcakes: In a bowl, sift flour, baking powder, baking soda and salt. Add cocoa powder for chocolate cupcakes and vanilla extract for vanilla cupcakes.

3. Cream butter and sugar in electric mixer with the mixer's flat beater on medium speed until mixture is light and airy.

4. Reduce mixing speed to low, add egg, mix well.

5. Gradually add dry ingredients (prepared in Step 2) and buttermilk, mix until batter is smooth.

6. Fill the cupcake liners. Bake for 10-12 minutes, or until cupcakes are springy to the touch and a toothpick inserted in cupcake's center comes out clean.

7. Remove from oven and cool on wire rack for 10 minutes.

8. Accessorize cupcakes: Remove cupcake foil and insert lollipop stick halfway through the center of each cupcake.

9. Wrap each lollipop cupcake in clear cellophane, tying with satin ribbon.

Peanut Butter and Jelly Cupcakes

~~~~~~~~~~~~~~~~~~~~~

Makes

~ 12 ~

Cupcakes

INGREDIENTS

2⅓ cups white flour

2 tablespoons baking powder

¼ teaspoon salt

½ cup butter, at room temperature

1⅓ cups sugar

5 tablespoons peanut butter

2 eggs

½ cup milk

2 tablespoons strawberry jam

Frosting:

½ cup peanut butter

2 tablespoons honey

2 tablespoons milk

4 tablespoons cream cheese

3 tablespoons high quality strawberry jam

Accessories for assembly:

Toothpicks topped with colorful animals

The secret to this wonderful cupcake is not to over-bake it. You want the cupcake to remain moist. When adding the jam to the batter, fold it in gently with a spoon, so that uneven lumps of jam will pop up and surprise you.

~~~~~~

PREPARATION

1. Preheat the oven to 325°F. Insert liners into medium cupcake pans.

2. Prepare cupcakes: In a bowl, sift flour, baking powder and salt.

3. Cream butter, sugar, and peanut butter in an electric mixer with the mixer's flat beater on medium speed until mixture is fluffy.

4. Reduce mixing speed to low, add eggs one at a time, mixing well.

5. Gradually add dry ingredients (prepared in Step 2) and milk, mix until batter is smooth.

6. With the help of a spoon, add jam, lightly mixing so chunks of fruit remain in the batter.

7. Fill the cupcake liners two-thirds full.

8. Bake for 20-25 minutes, or until cupcakes are springy to the touch and a toothpick inserted in cupcake's center comes out clean.

9. Remove from oven, cool on wire rack for 10 minutes.

10. Prepare frosting: In a bowl, cream peanut butter with honey, milk and cream cheese.

11. Spread a generous tablespoon of peanut butter frosting on each cupcake, top with teaspoonful of strawberry jam, finishing off by inserting animal topped toothpick.

Chocolate Mousse Madness Cupcakes

Makes
~ *12* ~
Cupcakes

INGREDIENTS

2½ cups white flour

1 tablespoon baking powder

¼ teaspoon salt

¼ teaspoon baking soda

3 tablespoons cocoa

½ cup butter, at room temperature

1 cup sugar

3 eggs

½ cup whole milk

Chocolate mousse:

2 cups dark chocolate

⅔ cup milk chocolate

3½ tablespoons cubed butter

3 eggs

1 tablespoon brandy

1¾ cups whipping cream

1½ tablespoons powdered sugar

This is my winning recipe for chocolate mousse. It's quick and easy to prepare and always comes out wonderfully. To prevent the cupcake from falling apart when filling with chocolate mousse, be sure not to scrape out too much of the cake. Drizzling a bit of mousse in the cupcake's center will be enough, as long as you are generous with the amount of mousse you top with.

PREPARATION

1. Preheat the oven to 325°F. Insert liners into medium cupcake pans.

2. Prepare cupcakes: In a bowl, sift flour, baking powder, salt, baking soda, and cocoa.

3. Cream butter and sugar in electric mixer with the mixer's flat beater on medium speed until mixture is light and airy.

4. Reduce mixing speed to low, add eggs one at a time, mixing well.

5. Gradually add dry ingredients (prepared in Step 2) and milk, mix until batter is smooth.

6. Fill the cupcake liners two-thirds full.

7. Bake for 20-25 minutes, or until cupcakes are springy to the touch and a toothpick inserted in cupcake's center comes out clean.

8. Remove from oven and cool on wire rack for 10 minutes.

9. With a serrated knife, slice about a ¼" off the top of each cupcake, reserving sliced portion. With a spoon, remove a bit of the cake's center to create a space for the chocolate mousse. Be careful not to remove sides or bottom of cupcakes.

10. Prepare chocolate mousse: In a bowl placed over a pot of hot water (double boiler), melt dark and milk chocolate. Once melted, add cubes of butter, mix into batter.

11. Add eggs one at a time while mixing constantly for about 2 minutes. Add brandy and continue mixing into a smooth batter. Remove from heat.

12. In a separate bowl, whip cream with powdered sugar into a soft cream.

13. Add 2 tablespoons of whipped cream into chocolate mixture and beat, then gently fold chocolate mixture into remaining whipped cream to achieve a smooth and airy mousse.

14. Make sure chocolate mixture is not too warm to prevent it from melting the cream. If too cold, the chocolate mixture will harden immediately.

15. Transfer mousse to pastry bag.

16. Assemble cupcakes: Insert chocolate mousse into hollow of cupcakes working your way up to create an even frosting. Refrigerate for half an hour to allow mousse to set and harden. Slice reserved cupcake tops in half with a sharp knife, diagonally attach to frosting like wings.

Mini-Me Marshmallow Cupcakes

~~~~~~~~~~~~~~~~~~~

Makes

~ 12 ~

Cupcakes

INGREDIENTS

2⅓ cups white flour

½ teaspoon baking powder

¼ teaspoon salt

¼ teaspoon baking soda

2 eggs

1 cup sugar

½ cup canola oil

½ cup sour cream

Frosting:

½ cup butter, at room temperature

1 tablespoon vanilla extract

1 cup powdered sugar

Garnish:

Mini marshmallows

The introduction of marshmallow into this basic and easy-to-prepare recipe is certainly what clinches the winning quality of these cupcakes among the kids. Mini-marshmallows are attached to the top of the cupcake with a bit of buttercream frosting. Of course, I also recommend letting the children play with the marshmallow topping to create additional cupcake designs.

~~~~~~~~~~~~~~~~~~~~~~~~~~~~~~~~~~~~~

PREPARATION

1. Preheat the oven to 325°F. Insert liners into medium cupcake pans.

2. Prepare cupcakes: In a bowl, sift flour, baking powder, salt, and baking soda.

3. Beat eggs and sugar in an electric mixer until mixture is white and fluffy.

4. Reduce mixing speed to low, add oil and half of dry ingredients (prepared in Step 2).

5. Add sour cream and remaining flour mixture, mix.

6. Fill the cupcake liners two-thirds full.

7. Bake for 20-25 minutes, or until cupcakes are springy to the touch and a toothpick inserted in cupcake's center comes out clean.

8. Remove from oven and cool on wire rack for 10 minutes.

9. Prepare frosting: With an electric mixer, beat butter with vanilla extract and powdered sugar until frosting is smooth.

10. With a spatula, spread 1 tablespoon of frosting ¼" thick on each cupcake, pressing mini marshmallows on top. To achieve symmetry, place first marshmallow in center of cupcake, working your way out in circles.

Toffee Square Cupcake Surprise

~~~~~~~~~~~~~~~~~~~~

Makes
~ *12* ~
Cupcakes

INGREDIENTS

40 toffee squares:

1 cup whipping cream

1/5 cup whole milk

1 cup + 2 tablespoons sugar

3½ tablespoons gluten

1½ cups salted butter

Pinch of sea salt

Cupcakes:

3 cups white flour

1 tablespoon baking powder

¼ teaspoon salt

¼ teaspoon baking soda

½ cup butter, at room temperature

1 cup brown sugar

3 eggs

¼ cup condensed milk

Toffee squares can be bought ready made, and I will admit that preparing them yourself requires effort, investment and careful attention to the various steps. However, these little toffee sweets are a treat in themselves and leftovers can be wrapped in cellophane like a lollipop and given out to friends and loved ones...if you can bear to part with them.

~~~~~~~~~~~~~~~~~~~~~~~~~~~~~~~~~~~~~~~

PREPARATION

1. Prepare toffee squares: In a saucepan, heat whipping cream, milk, sugar and gluten with 7 tablespoons butter until mixture reaches 225°F (you will need a candy thermometer for this). Mix continuously with wooden spoon. Batter needs to be thick and slightly caramelized.

2. Remove from heat, carefully add remaining butter (hold away from body), add salt, mix well, pour into small cake pan lined with parchment paper. Batter needs to be 1" thick, wrapped in parchment, and cooled on counter. (It's best not to refrigerate, since caramel absorbs moisture. But, if the weather is too hot, caramel won't harden).

3. When ready, cut into 1" by 1" squares. Preheat the oven to 325°F. Insert liners into medium cupcake pans.

4. Prepare cupcakes: In a bowl, sift flour, baking powder, salt and baking soda.

5. Cream butter and sugar in electric mixer with the mixer's flat beater on medium speed until mixture is light and airy. Reduce mixing speed to low, add eggs one at a time, mixing well.

6. Gradually add dry ingredients (prepared in Step 4) and concentrated milk, mix until incorporated into smooth batter.

7. Add toffee squares (prepared in Steps 1-3) to batter, continuing to mix by hand.

8. Fill the cupcake liners two-thirds full. Bake for 20-25 minutes, or until cupcakes are springy to the touch, and a toothpick inserted in centers comes out clean.

9. Remove from oven and cool on wire rack for 10 minutes.

Cupcake Celebrations
~~~~~~

Baby Shower Cupcakes

Wedding Cupcakes

Mini Mascarpone Birthday Cupcakes

Mini Chocolate Valentine Cupcakes

Chestnut Cupcakes

Gluten Free Passover Cupcakes

Anniversary Mini Cinnamon Cupcakes

White Christmas Cupcakes

Pumpkin Cupcakes

Baby Shower Cupcakes

~~~~~~~~~~~~~~~~~~~~~

Makes

~ *12* ~

Cupcakes

These cupcakes are a feast for the eyes and can serve as decorative (and tasty) centerpieces for the table at your baby shower. The cupcake recipe itself is basic, with most of the work going into frosting and decorating. Make sure to limit the amount of food coloring used in the frosting in order to achieve softer pastel colors.

~~~~~~

INGREDIENTS

3 cups white flour

1 tablespoon baking powder

¼ teaspoon salt

¼ teaspoon baking soda

½ cup butter, at room temperature

1 cup sugar

1 tablespoon vanilla extract

2 eggs

1½ cups buttermilk

Frosting:

½ cup butter, at room temperature

⅔ cup cream cheese

2 tablespoons coconut cream

2 cups powdered sugar

Pink and/or light blue food coloring

Garnish:

Pink and blue crystal sugar

Small sugar pacifiers

PREPARATION

1. Preheat the oven to 325°F. Insert liners into medium cupcake pans.

2. Prepare cupcakes: In a bowl, sift flour, baking powder, salt and baking soda.

3. Cream butter and sugar in electric mixer with the mixer's flat beater on medium speed. Add vanilla extract (scraping sides of bowl as needed), until mixture is light and airy.

4. Reduce mixing speed to low, add eggs one at a time, mixing well.

5. Gradually add dry ingredients (prepared in Step 2) and buttermilk, mixing until incorporated into a smooth batter. Fill the cupcake liners two-thirds full.

6. Bake for 20-25 minutes, or until cupcakes are springy to the touch and a toothpick inserted in cupcake's center comes out clean.

7. Remove from oven and cool on wire rack for 10 minutes.

8. Prepare frosting: In an electric mixer on low speed, cream butter, cream cheese, and coconut cream for about 2 minutes until texture is even and smooth.

9. Gradually add powdered sugar, continuing to beat 2-3 more minutes to achieve even and airy ready-to-use frosting.

10. Add a few drops of pink or blue food coloring, mix to achieve desired color. (I recommend starting with just a tiny bit of food coloring and adding as necessary.)

11. Transfer to pastry bag with a star shaped tip, applying frosting in a circular motion starting from edges and moving up towards center of cupcake.

12. Sprinkle with colorful sugar crystals and top with pacifier.

Wedding Cupcakes

~~~~~~~~~~~~~~~~~~~~

Makes
~ *12* ~
Cupcakes

These cupcakes are especially festive and elegant and may be offered as gifts to invited wedding guests, or to the newlyweds as a sweet gesture for their special day. The cupcakes can also be used in the seating arrangements, attaching cards with guests' names, or even as a substitute for a wedding cake. Most importantly, these cupcakes should be prepared with love and eaten with pleasure.

~~~~~~~~~~~~~~~~~~~~~~~~~~~~~~~~~~~~~~~

INGREDIENTS

3 cups white flour

¼ teaspoon salt

1 tablespoon baking powder

½ cup butter, at room temperature

1 cup vanilla sugar

1 tablespoon vanilla extract

2 eggs

1 cup whole milk

Frosting:

1 cup unsalted butter, at room temperature

1 cup Philadelphia cream cheese

4 cups powdered sugar

1 tablespoon citrus extract

Accessories for assembly:

White colored candies

Blue colored pastry roses

Bride and groom dolls

PREPARATION

1. Preheat the oven to 325°F. Insert liners into medium cupcake pans.

2. Prepare cupcakes: In a bowl, sift flour, salt and baking powder.

3. Cream butter and vanilla sugar in an electric mixer with the mixer's flat beater on medium speed. Add vanilla extract (scrape sides of bowl as needed), until mixture is light and airy.

4. Reduce mixing speed to low, add eggs one at a time, mixing well.

5. Gradually add dry ingredients (prepared in Step 2) and milk, mixing until incorporated and smooth batter is achieved.

6. Fill the cupcake liners two-thirds full.

7. Bake for 20-25 minutes, or until cupcakes are springy to the touch and a toothpick inserted in cupcake's center comes out clean.

8. Remove from oven, cool on wire rack for 10 minutes.

9. Prepare frosting: In an electric mixer cream butter and cream cheese on low speed for about 2 minutes, gradually adding powdered sugar and citrus extract. Continue mixing for 2-3 minutes until frosting is fluffy, even and ready to use.

10. Transfer frosting to pastry bag with a petal tip.

11. Pipe flowers onto the cupcakes, decorating with white candy sprinkles and blue sugar flowers. Place bride and groom doll on top.

Mini Mascarpone Birthday Cupcakes

~~~~~~~~~~~~~~~~~~~~

Makes

~ *42* ~

Mini cupcakes

These cupcakes serve as a colorful and original substitute for the traditional birthday cake. You'll see how easy it is to surprise your loved ones on their birthdays. I don't know of anyone (children and adults alike) who aren't completely won over by these fun and sophisticated cupcakes. Be sure to prepare enough for seconds.

~~~~~~

INGREDIENTS

3 cups white flour

1 tablespoon baking powder

¼ teaspoon salt

¼ teaspoon baking soda

½ cup butter, at room temperature

1¼ cups sugar

3 eggs

1 tablespoon vanilla extract

1 tablespoon thinly grated lemon zest

½ cup crème fraiche

Frosting:

⅘ cup mascarpone cheese

1¾ cups powdered sugar

2 tablespoons almond extract

Garnish:

Colorful sprinkles

PREPARATION

1. Preheat the oven to 325°F. Insert liners into mini cupcake pans.

2. Prepare cupcakes: In a bowl, sift flour, baking powder, baking soda and salt.

3. Cream butter and sugar in an electric mixer with the mixer's flat beater on medium speed until mixture is light and airy.

4. Reduce mixing speed to low, add eggs one at a time, mixing well.

5. Add vanilla extract and lemon zest. Mix well after each addition.

6. Gradually add dry ingredients (prepared in Step 2) and crème fraiche, mixing well until batter is smooth.

7. Fill the cupcake liners two-thirds full.

8. Bake for 20-25 minutes, or until cupcakes are springy to the touch and a toothpick inserted in cupcake's center comes out clean.

9. Remove from oven, cool on wire rack for 10 minutes.

10. Prepare frosting: Cream mascarpone cheese in an electric mixer on low speed for about 2 minutes.

11. Gradually add powdered sugar and almond extract, continuing to mix for 2-3 minutes to achieve a light, airy, ready-to-use frosting.

12. Transfer to pastry bag with a round tip, piping upwards from sides towards center. Sprinkle on colorful candies. Add small birthday candle if desired.

Mini Chocolate Valentine Cupcakes
~~~~~~~~~~~~~~~~~~~

Makes
~ *42* ~
Mini cupcakes

These sexy, romantic mini cupcakes have a dark chocolate taste that will explode in your mouth. The thick and creamy chocolate ganache frosting is topped with red heart-shaped candies. Anyone treated to these cupcakes as a Valentine's gift is bound to love you forever.
~~~~~~~~~~~~~~~~~~~~~~~~~~~~~~~~~~~~

INGREDIENTS

2½ cups white flour

½ teaspoon baking powder

¼ teaspoon salt

½ teaspoon baking soda

⅔ cup chopped dark chocolate

½ cup + 1 tablespoon butter, at room temperature

1⅓ cups sugar

2 eggs

½ cup sour cream

Frosting:

⅔ cup whipping cream

1 tablespoon vanilla extract

1⅓ cups dark chocolate, broken into cubes

Garnish:

Red heart candies

PREPARATION

1. Preheat the oven to 325°F. Insert liners into mini cupcake pans.

2. Prepare cupcakes: In a bowl, sift flour, baking powder, salt and baking soda.

3. In a bowl placed over a pot of hot water (double boiler), melt chocolate and mix until smooth. Remove from heat and cool.

4. Cream butter and sugar in an electric mixer with the mixer's flat beater on low speed until mixture is light and airy. Increase mixing speed to medium, adding eggs one at a time, mixing well. Continue mixing for about 1 minute.

5. Gradually add half of sour cream and half of dry ingredients (prepared in Step 2), mixing until incorporated into a smooth batter. Add remaining sour cream and flour mixture.

6. Reduce mixing speed to low, add melted chocolate and mix well until batter is smooth. Fill the cupcake liners two-thirds full.

7. Bake for about 10 minutes, or until cupcakes are springy to the touch and a toothpick inserted in cupcake's center comes out clean.

8. Remove from oven and cool on wire rack for 10 minutes.

9. Prepare frosting: In a small saucepan, heat whipping cream and vanilla extract just to boiling point.

10. Pour cream on cubed chocolate and wait about 1 minute for chocolate to melt. Whisk mixture in center of bowl until a thick and uniform ganache is formed. Cool for about 10 minutes.

11. Pour one tablespoon of ganache on each cupcake, sprinkle candy hearts on top.

Chestnut Cupcakes

~~~~~~~~~~~~~~~~~~~~~

Makes

~ *12* ~

Cupcakes

INGREDIENTS

3 cups white flour

1 tablespoon baking powder

¼ teaspoon salt

¼ teaspoon baking soda

½ cup butter, at room temperature

½ cup sugar

2 eggs

½ cup chestnut purée

⅓ cup dulce de leche

Frosting:

¼ cup + 2 tablespoons butter, at room temperature

¾ cup + 2 tablespoons chestnut purée

3½ tablespoons powdered sugar

1½ tablespoons rum

Garnish:

12 whole candied chestnuts

Chestnuts, with their delicately sweet warm scent always remind me of Christmas time. This is a wonderful and sweet recipe you will want to enjoy year round. It is important to use only slightly sweetened, quality chestnut purée. If the purée is very sweet, you may want to reduce the amount of sugar.

~~~~~~~~~~~~~~~~~~~~~~~~~~~~~~~~~~~~~~

PREPARATION

1. Preheat the oven to 325°F. Insert liners into medium cupcake pans.

2. Prepare cupcakes: In a bowl, sift flour, baking powder, baking soda, and salt.

3. Cream butter and sugar in an electric mixer with the mixer's flat beater on medium speed, until mixture is light and fluffy.

4. Reduce mixing speed to low, add eggs one at a time, add chestnut purée and dulce de leche, mixing well.

5. Gradually add dry ingredients (prepared in Step 2), mix well until incorporated into smooth batter. Fill the cupcake liners two-thirds full.

6. Bake for 20-25 minutes, or until cupcakes are springy to the touch and a toothpick inserted in cupcake's center comes out clean.

7. Remove from oven and cool on wire rack for 10 minutes.

8. Prepare frosting: Cream butter and chestnut purée with an electric mixer on low speed for about 2 minutes until frosting is smooth, add powdered sugar.

9. Towards the end, add rum and mix for about 1 more minute.

10. Place 1 tablespoon of frosting on each cupcake and garnish with 1 candied chestnut in center of each cupcake.

Gluten Free Passover Cupcakes

~~~~~~~~~~~~~~~~~~~~

Makes

~ 12 ~

Cupcakes

INGREDIENTS

2 cups almond flour (or thinly ground blanched almonds)

½ cup tapioca flour

⅓ cup potato flour

¼ teaspoon salt

¼ teaspoon baking soda

½ cup butter, at room temperature

1 cup sugar

2 eggs

1 tablespoon vanilla extract

1 cup buttermilk

According to Jewish tradition, eating wheat flour during Passover is forbidden as a reminder of when the Jewish people's exodus from Egypt didn't allow time for the bread to rise. Regardless of the holiday, this recipe is a healthy and no less tasty solution for anyone who doesn't eat gluten or for those who have removed wheat flour from their diets. Try this recipe – you'll be surprised at its success.

~~~~~~~~~~~~~~~~~~~~~~~~~~~~~~~~~~~~~~

PREPARATION

1. Preheat the oven to 325°F. Insert liners into medium cupcake pans.

2. In a bowl, sift almond flour, tapioca flour, potato flour, salt and baking soda.

3. Cream butter and sugar in the bowl of an electric mixer with the mixer's flat beater on medium speed until mixture is fluffy.

4. Reduce mixing speed to low, add eggs one at a time, add vanilla extract, mixing well.

5. Gradually add dry ingredients (prepared in Step 2) and buttermilk, mix until incorporated into smooth batter.

6. Fill the cupcake liners two-thirds full.

7. Bake for 20-25 minutes, or until cupcakes are springy to the touch and a toothpick inserted in cupcake's center comes out clean.

8. Remove from oven and cool on wire rack for 10 minutes.

9. Sprinkle powdered sugar on top of each cupcake for decoration.

Anniversary Mini Cinnamon Cupcakes

~~~~~~~~~~~~~~~~~~~~

Makes

~ *42* ~

Mini cupcakes

INGREDIENTS

3 cups white flour

1 tablespoon baking powder

¼ teaspoon baking soda

¼ teaspoon salt

3 tablespoons ground cinnamon

¼ teaspoon ground cloves

½ cup butter, at room temperature

¾ cup sugar

¼ cup cinnamon sugar

2 eggs

1 cup sour cream

Frosting:

¾ cup + 2 tablespoons cream cheese

1½ cups powdered sugar

2 tablespoons liquid cinnamon extract

Red food coloring

The cinnamon's dominant fragrance and sweet, woody flavor lend these cupcakes a romantic and tempting dimension especially befitting a romantic anniversary. Cinnamon has been attributed with powerful antiseptic qualities, and my grandmother swore that cinnamon dispels bad breath far more effectively than mint; all the more reason to celebrate the occasion with a kiss.

~~~~~~~~~~~~~~~~~~~~~~~~~~~~~~~~~~~~~

PREPARATION

1. Preheat the oven to 325°F. Insert liners into mini cupcake pans.

2. Prepare cupcakes: In a bowl, sift flour, baking powder, baking soda, salt, ground cinnamon and cloves.

3. Cream butter, sugar and cinnamon sugar in an electric mixer with the mixer's flat beater on medium speed until mixture is light and airy. Reduce mixing speed to low, add eggs one at a time, mixing well.

4. Gradually add dry ingredients (prepared in Step 2) and sour cream, mixing until incorporated into a smooth batter. Fill the cupcake liners two-thirds full.

5. Bake for 20-25 minutes, or until cupcakes are springy to the touch and a toothpick inserted in cupcake's center comes out clean.

6. Remove from oven and cool on wire rack for 10 minutes.

7. Prepare frosting: Beat cream cheese with an electric mixer on low speed for about 2 minutes.

8. Gradually add powdered sugar and cinnamon extract, continuing to mix for another 2-3 minutes until frosting is light and ready to use.

9. Add red food coloring for a bold color, mix well for a uniform color. Add more food coloring as needed.

10. Transfer to a pastry bag with a star tip, piping a snail in the center of cupcakes, leaving perimeters exposed.

White Christmas Cupcakes

~~~~~~~~~~~~~~~~~~~

Makes

~ 10 ~

Star cupcakes

INGREDIENTS

2½ cups white flour

1 tablespoon baking powder

⅓ teaspoon baking soda

¼ teaspoon salt

½ cup + 1 tablespoon butter, at room temperature

1 cup sugar

2 tablespoons brandy

2 eggs

½ cup crème fraiche

Frosting:

¾ cup + 2 tablespoons softened cream cheese

1½ cups powdered sugar

1 teaspoon lemon juice

1 tablespoon brandy

Garnish:

White sugar dough

Corn flour

Star-shaped cookie cutters

There is nothing like getting into the Christmas spirit by serving guests a personal Christmas cupcake decorated with frosting as white as snow. The star shaped muffin tins in which I bake these cupcakes add to the beauty and magical festivity of this holiday.

~~~~~~~~~~~~~~~~~~~~~~~~~~~~~~~~~~~~~~~

PREPARATION

1. Preheat the oven to 325°F. Insert liners into medium cupcake pans.

2. Prepare cupcakes: In a bowl, sift flour, baking powder, baking soda and salt.

3. Cream butter, sugar and brandy in an electric mixer on medium speed with the mixer's flat beater, until mixture is light and airy.

4. Reduce mixing speed to low, add eggs one at a time, mixing well.

5. Gradually add dry ingredients (prepared in Step 2) and crème fraiche, mixing until incorporated and batter is smooth. Fill the cupcake liners two-thirds full.

6. Bake for 20-25 minutes, or until cupcakes are springy to the touch and a toothpick inserted into cupcake's center comes out clean.

7. Remove from oven and cool on wire rack for 10 minutes.

8. Prepare frosting: With an electric mixer on low speed, beat cream cheese for about 2 minutes.

9. Gradually add powdered sugar, lemon juice and brandy, continuing to beat for 2-3 minutes until frosting is fluffy and ready to use.

10. Transfer frosting to pastry bag with a star-shaped tip. Pipe stars close together until tops of cupcakes are entirely covered.

11. Prepare garnish: Roll out prepared sugar dough (sprinkle corn flour on work area and rolling pin to prevent the dough from sticking). Roll dough out thin (¼") and cut out star-shaped cookies with help of cookie cutter.

12. Decorate cupcake with sugar dough stars.

Pumpkin Cupcakes

~~~~~~~~~~~~~~~~~~~

Makes

~ *12* ~

Cupcakes

INGREDIENTS

3 cups white flour

1 tablespoon baking powder

½ teaspoon baking soda

¼ teaspoon salt

¼ teaspoon nutmeg

1 cup butter, at room temperature

1½ cups sugar

2 eggs

One 15-ounce can pumpkin purée

Orange food coloring as needed

Garnish:

¾ cup + 2 tablespoons sugar dough

Orange food coloring

Sweet pumpkin spiced with nutmeg is an especially festive pleasure. To prepare the pumpkin garnish, I use sugar dough lightly dyed with orange food coloring. If you're an especially talented sculptor, this is your chance to show off your skills: sculpt a sugar dough spider, a skeleton, a witch or a jack-o-lantern.

~~~~~~

PREPARATION

1. Preheat the oven to 325°F. Insert liners into medium cupcake pans.

2. Prepare cupcakes: In a bowl sift four, baking powder, baking soda, salt and nutmeg.

3. Cream butter and sugar in an electric mixer with the mixer's flat beater on medium speed until mixture is fluffy. Reduce mixing speed to low, add eggs one at a time, mixing well.

4. Gradually add dry ingredients (prepared in Step 2) and pumpkin purée, mixing until incorporated into a smooth batter. Add orange food coloring as needed before baking, mix well.

5. The need to add food coloring to the batter depends on the natural color of the purée you used. In case the batter did not achieve the desired color from the purée alone, add a bit of the orange food coloring. It's always best to start with one or two drops, adding as needed.

6. Fill the cupcake liners two-thirds full. Bake 20-25 minutes, or until cupcakes are springy to the touch and a toothpick inserted in cupcake's center comes out clean Remove from oven and cool on wire rack for 10 minutes.

7. Prepare garnish: Roll sugar dough into a ball, press finger in center of ball to create a hollow, pouring a bit of orange food coloring into hollow. Close hollow and begin to knead ball from the outside in. Sprinkle powdered sugar or corn flour on work surface to prevent dough from sticking.

8. When a uniform color is achieved, make balls about 2" large, place on work surface, pressing each lightly to create indentation. With the help of a kitchen knife or toothpick, mark spaced lines from top center down towards bottom center. Finish by attaching a mint leaf by its stem to the top of the pumpkin. Place 1 sugar dough pumpkin on top of each cupcake.

A Cupcake to Your Health

~~~~~~~~~~~~~~~~~~~~~~~~~~~~~~~~~~~~~~~

Vegan Dark Chocolate Cupcakes

Whole Wheat Hazelnut Cupcakes

Semolina and Raisin Cupcakes

Gluten and Dairy Free Cupcakes

Poppy Seed Cupcakes

Granola Cupcakes

Lemon Yogurt Cupcakes

Green Tea Cupcakes

Gooseberry and Pumpkin Seed Cupcakes

Hazelnut-Honey Cupcakes

Lavender, Clove and Cinnamon Cupcakes

Black and White Sesame Cupcakes

Pomegranate Cupcakes

Quinoa-Walnut Cupcakes

Tahini, Linseed and Date Honey Cupcakes

Oatmeal-Macadamia Nut Cupcakes

Vegan Dark Chocolate Cupcakes

Makes

~ 12 ~

Cupcakes

INGREDIENTS

2 cups white flour

½ teaspoon baking soda

1 tablespoon baking powder

6 tablespoons cocoa powder

1 cup sugar

¼ teaspoon salt

¾ cup water

½ cup canola oil

Frosting:

1⅓ cups dark chocolate

2 tablespoons canola oil

½ cup powdered sugar

2 tablespoons Kahlua coffee liqueur

Garnish:

Dark chocolate shavings

This is an especially enjoyable low calorie chocolate recipe. This recipe is suited to anyone keeping kosher who is looking for dairy-free dessert alternatives, or for vegan or lactose intolerant guests who don't eat eggs and dairy products.

PREPARATION

1. Preheat the oven to 325°F. Insert liners into medium cupcake pans.

2. Prepare cupcakes: In a bowl, sift flour, baking soda, baking powder, cocoa, sugar and salt.

3. Transfer dry mixture to the bowl of an electric mixer, gradually adding water and oil, mixing well until incorporated.

4. Fill the cupcake liners two-thirds full.

5. Bake for 20-25 minutes, or until cupcakes are springy to the touch and a toothpick inserted in cupcake's center comes out clean.

6. Remove from oven and cool on wire rack for 10 minutes.

7. Prepare frosting: Melt chocolate in a bowl set over a pot of boiling water, (double boiler) mixing occasionally.

8. When the chocolate melts, add canola oil, powdered sugar and finally Kahlua to melted chocolate, beating until frosting is smooth.

9. Spread generously with spatula on each cupcake.

10. Garnish with chocolate shavings.

Whole Wheat Hazelnut Cupcakes
~~~~~~~~~~~~~~~~~~~~~

Makes

~ *12* ~

Cupcakes

I added whole wheat flour to these cupcakes for anyone interested in adopting a healthier diet. The advantage of whole wheat flour is not only nutritional (it contains fibers that assist in the breakdown of foods), but it also has a coarser texture, which gives you a denser cupcake. The addition of chopped walnuts adds to the rich flavor.

~~~~~~

INGREDIENTS

1 cup white flour

1½ cups whole wheat flour

1 tablespoon baking powder

¼ teaspoon nutmeg

¼ teaspoon salt

½ cup butter, at room temperature

1 cup brown sugar

2 eggs

1 cup whole milk

1 cup + 2 tablespoons peeled, coarsely chopped hazelnuts

5 tablespoons toasted, shredded coconut

Garnish:

3 tablespoons toasted shredded coconut

7 tablespoons hazelnuts

PREPARATION

1. Preheat the oven to 325°F. Insert liners into medium cupcake pans.

2. Prepare cupcakes: In a bowl, sift white flour, whole wheat flour, baking powder, nutmeg and salt.

3. Cream butter and brown sugar in the bowl of an electric mixer with the mixer's flat beater on medium speed until mixture is light and fluffy.

4. Reduce mixing speed to low, add eggs one at a time, mixing well.

5. Gradually add dry ingredients (prepared in Step 2) and whole milk, mix. Add hazelnuts and shredded coconut, mixing for 1 more minute until incorporated into a smooth batter.

6. Fill the cupcake liners two-thirds full.

7. Bake for 20-25 minutes, or until cupcakes are springy to the touch and a toothpick inserted in cupcake's center comes out clean.

8. Remove from oven and cool on wire rack for 10 minutes.

9. Prepare garnish: Sprinkle a bit of the shredded coconut and hazelnuts on each cupcake.

Semolina and Raisin Cupcakes
~~~~~~~~~~~~~~~~~~~~~

Makes
~ *12* ~
Cupcakes

INGREDIENTS

1½ cups white flour

1½ cups semolina

1 tablespoon baking powder

¼ teaspoon salt

½ cup butter, at room temperature

1 teaspoon vanilla extract

1 cup sugar

2 eggs

1½ cups buttermilk

½ cup dark raisins

Spiced syrup:

1 cup water

1½ cups sugar

2 anise stars

1 cinnamon stick

1 teaspoon allspice

Tasty semolina (also known as cream of wheat) tends to dry out the cupcakes after baking which is why I dip them in spiced sugar syrup, allowing all the wonderful flavors of the syrup to be absorbed and seep into the cakes. The result is a fragrant, sweet and sticky cupcake.
~~~~~~~~~~~~~~~~~~~~~~~~~~~~~~~~~~~~~~

PREPARATION

1. Preheat the oven to 325°F. Insert liners into medium cupcake pans.

2. Prepare cupcakes: In a bowl, sift flour, semolina, baking powder and salt.

3. Cream butter, vanilla extract, and sugar in the bowl of an electric mixer with the mixer's flat beater on medium speed, until mixture is light and airy.

4. Reduce mixing speed to low, add eggs one at a time, mixing well.

5. Gradually add dry ingredients (prepared in Step 2) and buttermilk, mixing well until incorporated into smooth batter.

6. Add raisins to batter, mixing well until batter is of even consistency. Fill the cupcake liners two-thirds full.

7. Bake for 20-25 minutes, or until cupcakes are springy to the touch and a toothpick inserted in cupcake's center comes out clean.

8. Remove from oven and peel off muffin liners. Do not cool, cupcake will first be immersed in syrup.

9. Prepare spiced syrup: Pour water, sugar and spices into a pot and bring to a boil while stirring. Allow sugar to dissolve without sticking to the bottom of the pot.

10. Reduce heat and continue cooking on low for about 10 minutes until syrup is formed. Drain liquid through sieve to remove spices.

11. Immerse cupcakes in spiced syrup for a few seconds each (cupcakes will absorb syrup better while still warm). Remove cupcakes from syrup with slotted spoon.

12. Cool on wire rack until liquid is absorbed.

Gluten and Dairy Free Cupcakes
~~~~~~~~~~~~~~~~~~

Makes
~ *12* ~
Cupcakes

The combination of various flours is the secret to this recipe. Each type of flour has its own qualities, complementing each of the other flours and creating a healthy and wonderfully flavorful cupcake.
~~~~~~~~~~~~~~~~~~~~~~~~~~~~~~~~~~~~~~~

INGREDIENTS

⅓ cup tapioca flour

½ cup rice flour

½ cup potato flour

½ cup corn flour

1½ cups ground almond powder (or thinly ground blanched almonds)

¼ teaspoon baking soda

¼ teaspoon salt

¾ cup soy milk

1 teaspoon almond extract

¾ cup sugar

⅓ cup canola oil

Glaze:

1 cup powdered sugar

1½ tablespoons lemon juice

PREPARATION

1. Preheat the oven to 325°F. Insert liners into medium cupcake pans.

2. Prepare cupcake: In a bowl, sift tapioca flour, rice flour, potato flour, corn flour, almond powder, baking soda and salt.

3. Beat milk, almond extract, and sugar in the bowl of an electric mixer with the mixer's flat beater on medium speed until mixture is light and airy.

4. Gradually add dry ingredients (prepared in Step 2) and canola oil, mixing well until incorporated into smooth batter. Cool for 1 hour. Fill the cupcake liners two-thirds full.

5. Bake for 20-25 minutes, or until cupcakes are springy to the touch and a toothpick inserted in cupcake's center comes out clean.

6. Remove from oven and cool on wire rack for 10 minutes.

7. Prepare glaze: Mix powdered sugar and lemon juice to achieve a consistent glaze, and spread on each cupcake.

Poppy Seed Cupcakes

~~~~~~~~~~~~~~~~~~~

Makes

~ 12 ~

Cupcakes

INGREDIENTS

2½ cups white flour

1½ teaspoons baking powder

½ teaspoon salt

½ cup + 2 tablespoons butter, at room temperature

½ cup sugar

1 tablespoon almond extract

2 eggs

½ cup ground poppy seeds

½ cup milk

Frosting:

¼ cup apricot neutral glaze (available in stores specializing in pastry making)

If unavailable, substitute by melting ¼ cup apricot jam with 1 tablespoon water over low heat.

2 tablespoons water

These cupcakes are a little less sweet than most of the other recipes, which is why I like eating them in the morning, rather than for dessert. I recommend grinding the poppy seeds just before use since once ground, their aroma is released. Thus, it is best to grind poppy seeds as close as possible to date of use.

~~~~~~

PREPARATION

1. Preheat the oven to 325°F. Insert liners into medium cupcake pans.

2. Prepare cupcakes: In a bowl, sift flour, baking powder and salt.

3. Cream butter, sugar and almond extract in the bowl of an electric mixer with the mixer's flat beater on medium speed until mixture is light and fluffy.

4. Reduce mixing speed to low, add eggs one at a time, mixing well.

5. Gradually add dry ingredients (prepared in Step 2), ground poppy seeds and milk, mixing well until incorporated into smooth batter.

6. Fill the cupcake liners two-thirds full.

7. Bake for 20-25 minutes, or until cupcakes are springy to the touch and a toothpick inserted in cupcake's center comes out clean.

8. Remove from oven and cool on wire rack for 10 minutes.

9. Prepare frosting: In a small saucepan, heat glaze with water, mixing well until glaze melts.

10. With a brush, spread a bit of the shiny glaze on each cupcake and serve.

Granola Cupcakes

~~~~~~~~~~~~~~~~~~~

Makes
~ 12 ~
Cupcakes

Oatmeal has high nutritional value and a low calorie count – the exact things recommended to maintain a balanced diet. In this recipe I use natural oatmeal, as opposed to toasted granola, although you may certainly use that as well. I also add sunflower seeds, raisins, and shredded coconut, all of which come together to create these winning granola cupcakes.

~~~~~~~~~~~~~~~~~~~~~~~~~~~~~~~~~~~~~~

INGREDIENTS

2½ cups white flour

1½ teaspoons baking powder

½ teaspoon salt

⅓ cup butter, at room temperature

½ cup brown sugar

1 tablespoon ground cinnamon

2 eggs

¼ cup canola oil

2 tablespoons molasses

2 tablespoons date honey

⅓ cup oatmeal

3 tablespoons small dark raisins

1½ tablespoons shredded coconut

3 tablespoons sunflower seeds

Frosting:

¼ cup honey

3 tablespoons water

PREPARATION

1. Preheat the oven to 325°F. Insert liners into medium cupcake pans.

2. Prepare cupcakes: In a bowl, sift flour, baking powder and salt.

3. In the bowl of an electric mixer, cream butter, brown sugar, and ground cinnamon on medium speed until mixture is light and fluffy.

4. Reduce mixing speed to low, add eggs one at a time, mixing well.

5. Gradually add dry ingredients (prepared in Step 2), canola oil, molasses, and date honey, mixing well until batter is of smooth consistency.

6. Add oats, raisins, coconut, and sunflower seeds to batter, mixing well until incorporated into mixture. Fill the cupcake liners two-thirds full.

7. Bake for 20-25 minutes, or until cupcakes are springy to the touch and a toothpick inserted in cupcake's center comes out clean.

8. Remove from oven and cool on wire rack for 10 minutes.

9. Prepare frosting: In a small saucepan, heat honey and water and mix. Brush cupcakes with a bit of the honey water syrup.

Lemon Yogurt Cupcakes

~~~~~~~~~~~~~~~~~~~~

Makes

~ 12 ~

Cupcakes

INGREDIENTS

3 cups white flour

1 tablespoon baking powder

¼ teaspoon baking soda

¼ teaspoon salt

½ cup butter, at room temperature

¾ cup sugar

Zest of two lemons

2 eggs

4 tablespoons lemon juice

1½ cups low-fat yogurt

Frosting:

1 cup white chocolate

¼ cup light plain yogurt

2 tablespoons lemon juice

This is an easy recipe that takes advantage of yogurt's natural acidity, complementing it with the freshness of the lemon. If you are really serious about that diet, you can forego the white chocolate frosting.

~~~~~~~~~~~~~~~~~~~~~~~~~~~~~~~~~~~~~

PREPARATION

1. Preheat the oven to 325°F. Insert liners into medium cupcake pans.

2. Prepare cupcakes: In a bowl, sift flour, baking powder, baking soda and salt.

3. Cream butter, sugar and lemon zest in the bowl of an electric mixer with the mixer's flat beater on medium speed, beating until mixture is light and airy.

4. Reduce mixing speed to low, add eggs one at a time, add lemon juice, mixing well.

5. Gradually add dry ingredients (prepared in Step 2) and yogurt, mixing well until smooth batter is achieved. Fill the cupcake liners two-thirds full.

6. Bake for 20-25 minutes, or until cupcakes are springy to the touch and a toothpick inserted in cupcake's centers comes out clean.

7. Remove from oven and cool on wire rack for 10 minutes.

8. Prepare frosting: In a bowl placed over a pot with hot water (double boiler), melt white chocolate, mixing until consistent texture is achieved.

9. Add yogurt and lemon juice to melted chocolate and mix.

10. Spread a heaping tablespoon of white chocolate-lemon-yogurt ganache on each cupcake.

Green Tea Cupcakes

~~~~~~~~~~~~~~~~~~~~

Makes

~ *12* ~

Cupcakes

INGREDIENTS

3 cups white flour

1 tablespoon baking powder

¼ teaspoon baking soda

¼ teaspoon salt

½ cup butter, at room temperature

1 cup sugar

2 eggs

1 cup tepid green tea (without leaves)

Glaze:

1 egg white

1½ cups powdered sugar

1 teaspoon lemon juice

Green food coloring

Garnish:

2 tablespoons green tea leaves

Many studies have linked the drinking of green tea with the prevention of several diseases. Green tea helps strengthen the immune system, improve digestion, and heightens feelings of energy and usefulness.

~~~~~~

PREPARATION

1. Preheat the oven to 325°F. Insert liners into medium cupcake pans.

2. Prepare cupcakes: In a bowl, sift flour, baking powder, baking soda and salt.

3. Cream butter and sugar in the bowl of an electric mixer with the mixer's flat beater on medium speed, until mixture is light and airy.

4. Reduce mixing speed to low, add eggs one at a time, mixing well.

5. Gradually add dry ingredients (prepared in Step 2) and green tea, mixing well until batter is smooth. Fill the cupcake liners two-thirds full.

6. Bake for 20-25 minutes, or until cupcakes are springy to the touch and a toothpick inserted in cupcake's center comes out clean.

7. Remove from oven and cool on wire rack for 10 minutes.

8. Prepare glaze: In a bowl, beat egg white, gradually adding powdered sugar while continuing to beat into a thick and shiny batter.

9. Add lemon juice while continuing to beat.

10. Add a bit of green food coloring until pale green shade is achieved.

11. Place one tablespoon of glaze on each cupcake, sprinkling a few green tea leaves on top.

Gooseberry and Pumpkin Seed Cupcakes

~~~~~~~~~~~~~~~~~~~

Makes
~ *12* ~
Cupcakes

This cupcake is more of an energy snack than dessert and can replace breakfast or refuel energy lost during strenuous exercise. And its simply fantastic taste is further improved by the addition of gooseberries, also known as red currant.
~~~~~~~~~~~~~~~~~~~~~~~~~~~~~~~~~~~~~~

INGREDIENTS

2½ cups white flour

1½ teaspoons baking powder

½ teaspoon salt

½ cup butter, at room temperature

1 tablespoon vanilla extract

1 cup molasses

4 eggs

½ cup dried gooseberries

7 tablespoons shelled pumpkin seeds, unroasted

PREPARATION

1. Preheat the oven to 325°F. Insert liners into medium cupcake pans.

2. Prepare cupcakes: In a bowl, sift flour, baking powder and salt.

3. Cream butter and vanilla extract in the bowl of an electric mixer with the mixer's flat beater for about 1 minute, add molasses, add eggs one at a time, mixing well.

4. Gradually add dry ingredients (prepared in Step 2), mix until incorporated into smooth batter.

5. Add berries and pumpkin seeds to batter, mixing until consistency is smooth.

6. Fill the cupcake liners two-thirds full.

7. Bake for 20-25 minutes, or until cupcakes are springy to the touch and a toothpick inserted in cupcake's center comes out clean.

8. Remove from oven and cool on wire rack for 10 minutes.

Hazelnut-Honey Cupcakes

~~~~~~~~~~~~~~~~~~~~~~

Makes

~ 12 ~

Cupcakes

INGREDIENTS

3 cups white flour

1½ teaspoons baking powder

½ cup fine hazelnut powder

½ teaspoon salt

½ cup butter, at room temperature

1 tablespoon vanilla extract

½ cup sugar

2 eggs

½ cup honey

1 cup buttermilk

¾ cup coarsely chopped unroasted hazelnuts.

Frosting:

½ cup butter, at room temperature

4 tablespoons mascarpone cheese

2 tablespoons honey

2 cups powdered sugar

48 chopped hazelnuts

I love using orange blossom honey in this recipe because of its light color and delicate flavor that complements the dominant taste of the hazelnuts. Hazelnuts, by the way, are rich in natural oils, nutritional fibers, proteins, vitamin E and iron.

~~~~~~

PREPARATION

1. Preheat the oven to 325°F. Insert liners into medium cupcake pans.

2. Prepare cupcakes: In a bowl, sift flour, baking powder, hazelnut powder and salt.

3. Cream butter, vanilla extract and sugar in the bowl of an electric mixer with the mixer's flat beater on medium speed until mixture is light and airy.

4. Reduce mixing speed to low, add eggs one at a time, add honey, mixing well.

5. Gradually add dry ingredients (prepared in Step 2) and buttermilk, mix until batter is smooth.

6. Add chopped hazelnuts to batter and mix until incorporated.

7. Fill the cupcake liners two-thirds full.

8. Bake for 20-25 minutes, or until cupcakes are springy to the touch and a toothpick inserted in cupcake's center comes out clean.

9. Remove from oven and cool on wire rack for 10 minutes.

10. Prepare frosting: With an electric mixer on low speed, cream butter, mascarpone cheese, and honey for about 2 minutes until texture achieves smooth consistency.

11. Gradually add powdered sugar and continue beating for another 2-3 minutes to achieve light and airy ready-to-use frosting.

12. Place a generous tablespoon of frosting on each cupcake, topping each with 4 chopped hazelnuts, and drizzling with a bit of honey.

Lavender, Clove and Cinnamon Cupcakes

~~~~~~~~~~~~~~~~~~~~

Makes

~ *12* ~

Cupcakes

INGREDIENTS

3 cups white flour

1 tablespoon baking powder

¼ teaspoon baking soda

¼ teaspoon salt

1½ tablespoons ground cinnamon

1 teaspoon ground cloves

½ cup butter, at room temperature

1 cup sugar

3 eggs

1 tablespoon dried lavender flowers

Glaze:

1½ tablespoons lemon juice

1 cup powdered sugar

Purple food coloring

Garnish:

2 tablespoons lavender leaves

Lavender lends a floral, slightly sweet and elegant flavor to most dishes. For most cooking applications it is the dried buds (also referred to as flowers) of lavender that are used as only the buds contain the essential oil of lavender, which is where both the scent and flavor of lavender are best derived.

~~~~~~~~~~~~~~~~~~~~~~~~~~~~~~~~~~~~

PREPARATION

1. Preheat the oven to 325°F. Insert liners into medium cupcake pans.

2. Prepare cupcakes: In a bowl, sift flour, baking powder, baking soda, salt, ground cinnamon and ground cloves.

3. Cream butter and sugar in the bowl of an electric mixer with the mixer's flat beater on medium speed until mixture is light and airy.

4. Reduce mixing speed to low, add eggs one at a time, mixing well.

5. Gradually add dry ingredients (prepared in Step 2) and lavender flowers mixing well until incorporated into smooth batter. Fill the cupcake liners two-thirds full.

6. Bake for 20-25 minutes, or until cupcakes are springy to the touch and a toothpick inserted in cupcake's center comes out clean.

7. Remove from oven and cool on wire rack for 10 minutes.

8. Prepare glaze: Pour lemon juice into a bowl, adding powdered sugar. Mix until glaze is smooth.

9. Add a bit of purple food coloring and mix. Add lemon juice as needed.

10. Spread glaze on each cupcake and sprinkle with lavender leaves.

Black and White Sesame Cupcakes

~~~~~~~~~~~~~~~~~~~

Makes

~ 12 ~

Cupcakes

INGREDIENTS

3 cups white flour

1 tablespoon baking powder

¼ teaspoon baking soda

¼ teaspoon salt

½ cup butter, at room temperature

1 cup sugar

3 eggs

3 tablespoons black sesame seeds

3 tablespoons white sesame seeds

½ cup soy milk

Frosting:

½ cup white chocolate

1 cup softened cream cheese

3½ tablespoons melted butter

1 teaspoon vanilla extract

1 tablespoon white sesame seeds

1 tablespoon black sesame seeds

This is both an impressive and attractive cupcake. Before using, I toast white sesame seeds for about 1 minute in a hot pan, since the toasting releases the natural oils in the sesame seeds, bolstering their taste.

~~~~~~

PREPARATION

1. Preheat the oven to 325°F. Insert liners into medium cupcake pans.

2. Prepare cupcakes: In a bowl, sift flour, baking powder, baking soda and salt.

3. In the bowl of an electric mixer with the mixer's flat beater on medium speed, cream butter and sugar until mixture is light and fluffy.

4. Reduce mixing speed to low, add eggs one at a time, mixing well.

5. Gradually add dry ingredients (prepared in Step 2), black and white sesame seeds, and soy milk, mixing until incorporated into smooth batter. Fill the cupcake liners two-thirds full.

6. Bake for 20-25 minutes, or until cupcakes are springy to the touch and a toothpick inserted in cupcake's center comes out clean.

7. Remove from oven and cool on wire rack for 10 minutes.

8. Prepare frosting: In a bowl placed over a pot of hot water (double boiler), melt white chocolate and mix until blended in texture. (Chocolate can also be melted in microwave.)

9. In a bowl, mix cream cheese with melted butter, adding vanilla extract and both white and black sesame seeds.

10. Add melted white chocolate and continue stirring to achieve smooth frosting.

11. Spread heaping tablespoon of frosting on each cupcake, keeping refrigerated after use.

Pomegranate Cupcakes

~~~~~~~~~~~~~~~~~~~

Makes

~ *12* ~

Cupcakes

INGREDIENTS

2½ cups white flour

1½ teaspoons baking powder

½ teaspoon salt

½ cup butter, at room temperature

1 cup sugar

1 tablespoon grenadine syrup

2 eggs

½ cup pomegranate juice

Frosting:

⅔ cup cream cheese

3½ tablespoons butter at room temperature

3½ tablespoons powdered sugar

1 tablespoon freshly squeezed lemon juice

Garnish:

½ cup pomegranate seeds

The pomegranate is rich in minerals, iron and antioxidants, and research has even tied it to aging prevention. Regardless of all the pomegranate folklore, I am simply sold on its sweet and sour taste, along with its explosive texture. In season, I try to eat as much of it as possible.

~~~~~~~~~~~~~~~~~~~~~~~~~~~~~~~~~~~~~~

PREPARATION

1. Preheat the oven to 325°F. Insert liners into medium cupcake pans.

2. Prepare cupcakes: In a bowl, sift flour, baking powder and salt.

3. Cream butter, sugar, and grenadine syrup in the bowl of an electric mixer with the mixer's flat beater on medium speed until mixture is light and airy.

4. Reduce mixing speed to low, add eggs one at a time, mixing well.

5. Gradually add dry ingredients (prepared in Step 2) and pomegranate juice, mixing well until batter is smooth. Fill the cupcake liners two-thirds full.

6. Bake for 20-25 minutes, or until cupcakes are springy to the touch and a toothpick inserted in cupcake's center comes out clean.

7. Remove from oven and cool on wire rack for 10 minutes.

8. Prepare frosting: With an electric mixer on slow speed, beat cream cheese and butter for about 2 minutes.

9. Gradually add powdered sugar and lemon juice, continuing to beat for another 2-3 minutes until frosting is light and ready to use.

10. With the help of a spatula, spread frosting ½" thick on top of each cupcake

11. To garnish, sprinkle pomegranate seeds on frosting.

12. Here is a tip for selecting a good pomegranate: light pink fruit is sweeter, while the bolder red fruits are sourer. I prefer using fresh pomegranate juice prepared in a juicer. First the fruit's crown and end (where it connects to the branch) must be cut off. After washing the fruit, slice in two and juice.

Quinoa-Walnut Cupcakes
~~~~~~~~~~~~~~~~~~~~

Makes
~ *12* ~
Cupcakes

INGREDIENTS

Quinoa:

1 tablespoon canola oil

½ cup quinoa

¾ cup water

Cupcakes:

2½ cups white flour

1½ teaspoons baking powder

½ teaspoon salt

½ cup butter, at room temperature

1 cup sugar

3 tablespoons maple syrup

3 eggs

1 cup cold cooked quinoa

1 cup coarsely chopped walnuts

Quinoa has high nutritional value and is rich in all the essential amino acids, affording it a high level of protein. Quinoa is also rich in nutritional fibers, phosphor, iron and magnesium. In addition, quinoa doesn't contain gluten and is therefore suitable for those suffering from celiac, a gluten intolerance (although in this recipe, I have also made use of flour). Quinoa's combination with walnuts aids in the lowering of "bad" cholesterol, and helps in the prevention of heart disease, earning this cupcake a place of honor on the list of healthy recipes.
~~~~~~~~~~~~~~~~~~~~~~~~~~~~~~~~~~~~~

PREPARATION

1. Prepare quinoa: In a medium pot, heat canola oil for about 1 minute, add quinoa and stir for about 1 minute.

2. Add water, bring to a boil, then lower heat and cover pot. Cook over low heat for about 8 minutes until quinoa has absorbed all the water.

3. Turn off heat and leave pot covered for about 5 more minutes. When ready, transfer to a bowl to cool completely.

4. Preheat the oven to 325°F. Insert liners into medium cupcake pans.

5. Prepare cupcakes: In a bowl, sift flour, baking powder and salt.

6. Cream butter, sugar and maple syrup in the bowl of an electric mixer with the mixer's flat beater on medium speed until mixture is light and airy.

7. Reduce mixing speed to low, add eggs one at a time, mixing well.

8. Gradually add dry ingredients (prepared in Step 5), mixing until incorporated into smooth batter.

9. Add cooked quinoa and chopped walnuts to batter, mixing well. Fill the cupcake liners two-thirds full.

10. Bake for 20-25 minutes, or until cupcakes are springy to the touch, and a toothpick inserted in cupcake's center comes out clean.

11. Remove from oven and cool on wire rack for 10 minutes.

Tahini, Linseed and Date Honey Cupcakes

~~~~~~~~~~~~~~~~~~~~

Makes
~ *12* ~
Cupcakes

The combination of tahini (made from sesame seeds) and date honey (also known as silan) lends the cakes a flavor reminiscent of the Oriental treat *halva*. The addition of Omega 3 rich flax seeds (said to aid in lowering cholesterol) adds bite and texture to the cakes.

~~~~~~

INGREDIENTS

½ cup white flour

¾ cup rye flour

1 cup whole wheat flour

1 tablespoon baking powder

¼ teaspoon salt

½ cup butter, at room temperature

⅓ cup brown sugar

¾ cup date honey

2 eggs

5 tablespoons flax seeds

½ cup raw tahini

⅓ cup water

Garnish:

Date honey

PREPARATION

1. Preheat the oven to 325°F. Insert liners into medium cupcake pans.

2. In a bowl, sift white flour, rye flour, whole wheat flour, baking powder and salt.

3. Cream butter, brown sugar and date honey in the bowl of an electric mixer with the mixer's flat beater on medium speed until mixture is light and fluffy.

4. Reduce mixing speed to low, add eggs one at a time, mixing well.

5. Gradually add dry ingredients (prepared in Step 2), flax, tahini and water, mixing until incorporated into smooth batter. Fill the cupcake liners two-thirds full.

6. Bake for 20-25 minutes, or until cupcakes are springy to the touch and a toothpick inserted in cupcake's center comes out clean.

7. Remove from oven and cool on wire rack for 10 minutes.

8. Garnish top of each cupcake with a bit of date honey and serve.

Oatmeal-
Macadamia Nut
Cupcakes

~~~~~~~~~~~~~~~~~~

Makes

~ *12* ~

Cupcakes

INGREDIENTS

2 cups whole wheat flour

1 tablespoon baking powder

¼ teaspoon salt

½ cup Quaker oats

½ cup butter, at room temperature

1 cup brown sugar

2 eggs

1 cup milk

3 tablespoons macadamia nuts

This is the perfect cupcake to accompany coffee. It's rich, dense and filled with these wonderful nuts to which I am completely addicted.

~~~~~~

PREPARATION

1. Preheat the oven to 325°F. Insert liners into medium cupcake pans.

2. In a bowl, sift flour, baking powder and salt. Add Quaker oats and mix.

3. Cream butter and sugar in the bowl of an electric mixer with the mixer's flat beater on medium speed until mixture is light and fluffy.

4. Reduce mixing speed to low, add eggs one at a time, mixing well.

5. Gradually add dry ingredients (prepared in Step 2) and milk, mixing until incorporated into smooth batter. Add macadamia nuts and mix.

6. Fill the cupcake liners two-thirds full.

7. Bake for 20-25 minutes, or until cupcakes are springy to the touch, and a toothpick inserted in cupcake's center comes out clean.

8. Remove from oven and cool on wire rack for 10 minutes.

Cupcakes for Connoisseurs

~~~~~~

Crème Brulée Cupcakes

Tiramisu Cupcakes

Top Hat Cupcakes

Coffee Whiskey Cupcakes

Marzipan Cupcakes

Carrot, Ginger and Cardamom Cupcakes

Rose Cupcakes

Raspberry Vodka Cupcakes

Plum and Port Cupcakes

Nectarine Cupcakes

Tropical Cupcakes

Pavlova Cupcakes

Campari Grapefruit Cupcakes

Pistachio and White Chocolate Cupcakes

Upside-Down Apple Tatin Cupcakes

Vanilla Cream Puff Cupcakes

Crème Brulée Cupcakes
~~~~~~~~~~~~~~~~~~~~~~

Makes

~ 10 ~

Cupcakes

INGREDIENTS

3 cups white flour

1 tablespoon baking powder

¼ teaspoon salt

½ cup butter, at room temperature

1 cup sugar

1 tablespoon vanilla extract

2 eggs

1½ cups buttermilk

Frosting:

1 vanilla bean

2 cups milk

2 cups heavy cream

1 cup + 2 tablespoons sugar

8 egg yolks

5 tablespoons corn flour

This cupcake is baked in individual ramekins, on top of which rich natural vanilla frosting is spread. I recommend burning the caramel just before serving (*brulée* means burnt in French), in order to impress your guests with a hard caramel crust. If prepared too far in advance, the caramel melts and loses its crunch.
~~~~~~

PREPARATION

1. Preheat the oven to 325°F.

2. Prepare cupcakes: In a bowl, sift flour, baking powder and salt.

3. In the bowl of an electric mixer with the mixer's flat beater, cream butter, sugar and vanilla extract on medium speed until mixture is light and fluffy.

4. Reduce mixing speed to low, add eggs one at a time, mixing well.

5. Gradually add dry ingredients (prepared in Step 2) and buttermilk, mixing until blended into smooth batter.

6. Line individual ramekins (4" in diameter) with appropriate sized liners (if liners are unavailable, butter well and bake directly in ramekin), filling each two-thirds full.

7. Bake for 20-25 minutes, or until cupcakes are springy to the touch and a toothpick inserted in cupcake's center comes out clean.

8. Remove from oven and cool on wire rack for 10 minutes.

9. Prepare frosting: Cut vanilla bean in half length-wise, scraping the beans out with a knife.

10. Pour milk, cream, vanilla bean, and half the amount of sugar into a saucepan.

11. In a bowl, whisk egg yolks and remaining sugar, adding corn flour.

12. When the milk mixture boils, pour small amount into egg mixture and mix. Repeat step twice.

(continued on page 114)

(continued from page 112)

Garnish:

demerara sugar

13. Return mixture to saucepan and continue cooking on low heat while stirring constantly until texture is creamy and thick.

14. Remove from heat, transfer to a bowl and cover, allowing plastic wrap to touch top layer of cream to prevent film from forming. Cool and transfer to refrigerator.

15. When cream is completely cooled, remove wrap and whisk to create smooth frosting. Spread even ½" thick layer of frosting on each cupcake, and freeze for 1 hour.

16. Prepare garnish: Remove from freezer, generously sprinkling frosting with demerara sugar, lightly shaking off excess sugar.

17. With the use of a hand-held torch, gently scorch sugar to achieve hardened caramel. Be careful not to burn muffin liners by either removing liners completely, or burning the sugar in the center only.

18. Serve immediately after burning sugar.

19. All steps preceding burning may be done in advance, refrigerating cupcakes until it is time to harden the caramel.

Tiramisu Cupcakes

~~~~~~~~~~~~~~~~~~~

Makes

~ **12** ~

Cupcakes

INGREDIENTS

3 cups white flour

1 tablespoon baking powder

¼ teaspoon salt

½ cup butter, at room temperature

1 cup sugar

3 tablespoons Kahlua coffee liqueur

2 eggs

½ cup mascarpone cheese

¼ cup concentrated espresso

Frosting:

2 separated eggs

3 tablespoons sugar

⅔ cup mascarpone cheese

1¼ tablespoons Kahlua coffee liqueur

Garnish:

½ cup cocoa powder

One bite of this cupcake and you'll know what it means to enjoy *la dolce vita* (sweet life). Inspired by the famous Italian dessert, these tiramisu cupcakes will seduce you with the aromatic scent of coffee and the lovely texture of mascarpone cheese.

~~~~~~

PREPARATION

1. Preheat the oven to 325°F. Insert liners into medium cupcake pans.

2. Prepare cupcakes: In a bowl, sift flour, baking powder and salt.

3. In the bowl of an electric mixer with the mixer's flat beater on medium speed, cream butter, sugar and Kahlua until mixture is light and fluffy.

4. Reduce mixing speed to low, add eggs one at a time, mixing well.

5. Gradually add dry ingredients (prepared in Step 2), mascarpone and espresso, mixing well until blended into smooth batter. Fill the cupcake liners two-thirds full.

6. Bake for 20-25 minutes, or until cupcakes are springy to the touch and a toothpick inserted in cupcake's center comes out clean.

7. Remove from oven and cool on wire rack for 10 minutes.

8. Prepare frosting: Beat yolks and sugar into a light and fluffy mixture. Add mascarpone and mix until texture is smooth.

9. In a clean bowl, beat egg whites until stiff. Beat ⅓ of egg whites into cheese mixture.

10. Fold the remaining egg whites into mixture, adding coffee liqueur and mixing.

11. Place 1 heaping tablespoon of mascarpone frosting on each cupcake.

12. Sprinkle cocoa powder using dense sifter.

Top Hat Cupcakes
~~~~~~~~~~~~~~~~~~~

Makes
~ *12* ~
Cupcakes

INGREDIENTS

3 cups white flour

1 tablespoon baking powder

¼ teaspoon salt

½ cup butter, at room temperature

1 tablespoon vanilla extract

1 cup sugar

2 eggs

1½ cups buttermilk

Meringue:

8 egg whites

2¼ cups sugar

¼ teaspoon cream of tartar

Garnish:

2 cups dark chocolate

3 tablespoons canola oil

This recipe demands a bit more preparation time, yet the work pays off, resulting in a velvety chocolate cupcake with an impressive chocolate coated peak of meringue frosting. Undoubtedly worth the effort!
~~~~~~

PREPARATION

1. Preheat the oven to 325°F. Insert liners into medium cupcake pans.

2. Prepare cupcakes: In a bowl, sift flour, baking powder and salt.

3. In the bowl of an electric mixer with the mixer's flat beater, cream butter, vanilla extract, and sugar on medium speed until mixture is light and fluffy.

4. Reduce mixing speed to low, add eggs one at a time, mixing well.

5. Gradually add dry ingredients (prepared in Step 2) and buttermilk, mixing until blended into smooth batter. Fill the cupcake liners two-thirds full.

6. Bake for 20-25 minutes, or until cupcakes are springy to the touch and a toothpick inserted in cupcake's center comes out clean.

7. Remove from oven and cool on wire rack for 10 minutes.

8. Prepare meringue: Whisk egg whites, sugar, and cream of tartar in a bowl placed over a pot of hot water (double boiler), constantly mixing for about 5 minutes until texture is blended and mixture is hot to the touch (be sure not to cook eggs).

9. Transfer to bowl of electric mixer, beat on high until mixture has completely cooled and meringue is completely set.

10. Transfer meringue to pastry bag with round ⅜" tip, piping from sides of cupcakes up towards centers in a snail shape. Freeze for 30 minutes.

11. Prepare garnish: Melt chocolate and oil in a bowl placed over a pot of hot water (double boiler) until texture is smooth. Cool.

12. Place cupcakes on screen over a pan, gently ladling chocolate above. Chocolate will harden as it comes in contact with frozen meringue, which is why this step must be done fairly quickly and in a single step.

Coffee Whiskey Cupcakes
~~~~~~~~~~~~~~~~~~~

Makes
~ *12* ~
Cupcakes

INGREDIENTS

2½ cups white flour

1 tablespoon baking powder

¼ teaspoon salt

½ cup butter, at room temperature

1 cup sugar

2 eggs

½ cup concentrated espresso

Frosting:

½ cup water

1 cup sugar

7 egg yolks

1½ cups cubed butter, at room temperature

5 tablespoons concentrated espresso

2 tablespoons whiskey

Garnish:

Roasted coffee beans, coarsely chopped

PREPARATION

1. Preheat the oven to 325°F. Insert liners into medium cupcake pans.

2. Prepare cupcakes: In a bowl, sift flour, baking powder and salt.

3. In the bowl of an electric mixer with the mixer's flat beater on medium speed, cream butter and sugar until mixture is light and fluffy.

4. Reduce mixing speed to low, add eggs one at a time, mixing well.

5. Gradually add dry ingredients (prepared in Step 2) and espresso, mixing until blended into smooth batter. Fill the cupcake liners two-thirds full.

6. Bake for 20-25 minutes, or until cupcakes are springy to the touch and a toothpick inserted in cupcake's center comes out clean.

7. Remove from oven and cool on wire rack for 10 minutes.

8. Prepare frosting: In a small saucepan, warm water and sugar over low heat, cooking until syrup is achieved.

9. In the bowl of an electric mixer, beat egg yolks, gradually adding sugar syrup and continuing to beat until mixture has cooled completely.

10. Whisk cubed butter, espresso and whiskey into mixture.

11. Transfer frosting to a pastry bag, piping short porcupine tipped bursts.

12. Garnish with roasted coffee beans and serve.

Marzipan Cupcakes

~~~~~~~~~~~~~~~~~

Makes

~ *12* ~

Cupcakes

INGREDIENTS

1½ cups almond flour (or thinly ground blanched almonds)

1½ cups white flour

1 tablespoon baking powder

¼ teaspoon salt

½ cup butter, at room temperature

1 cup brown sugar

1½ teaspoons almond extract

3 eggs

1 cup milk

Frosting:

1¾ cups marzipan

2 tablespoons corn flour

1 beaten egg white

If you are mad about marzipan, this is the cupcake for you. Go as crazy as you like with the marzipan frosting, creating whatever shapes your heart desires.

~~~~~~~~~~~~~~~~~~~~~~~~~~~~~~~~~~~~~

PREPARATION

1. Preheat the oven to 325°F. Insert liners into medium cupcake pans.

2. Prepare cupcakes: In a bowl, sift both flours, baking powder and salt.

3. In the bowl of an electric mixer with the mixer's flat beater, cream butter, sugar, and almond extract on medium speed until mixture is light and fluffy.

4. Reduce mixing speed to low, add eggs one at a time, mixing well.

5. Gradually add dry ingredients (prepared in Step 2) and milk, mixing until blended into a smooth batter. Fill the cupcake liners two-thirds full.

6. Bake for 20-25 minutes, or until cupcakes are springy to the touch and a toothpick inserted in cupcake's center comes out clean.

7. Remove from oven and cool on wire rack for 10 minutes.

8. Prepare frosting: Using a rolling pin, roll out marzipan ¼" thick, sprinkling a bit of corn flour on work surface and rolling pin to prevent marzipan from sticking.

9. Cut out circles the size of cupcakes, with the help of a knife draw lines crosswise on each circle.

10. With a pastry brush, spread a thin layer of egg white on each cupcake. The egg white will help the marzipan adhere to the cakes. Place marzipan circle on top of each cupcake and serve.

Carrot, Ginger and Cardamom Cupcakes

~~~~~~~~~~~~~~~~~~~~

Makes
~ 12 ~
Cupcakes

INGREDIENTS

3 cups white flour

1 tablespoon baking powder

¼ teaspoon salt

½ teaspoon ground ginger

1 teaspoon ground cardamom

¼ teaspoon baking soda

½ cup butter, at room temperature

1 cup brown sugar

2 eggs

¼ cup orange juice

1⅓ cups shredded carrots

Frosting:

3½ tablespoons butter, at room temperature

½ cup + 2½ tablespoons cream cheese

¼ teaspoon cardamom

1 teaspoon orange zest

½ cup powdered sugar

1 tablespoon lemon juice

This is a sweet and sticky carrot cupcake. Don't give up on the cardamom - it's a great spice that naturally combines well with coffee, tea and a whole variety of sweet and savory dishes, always adding a wonderfully unique flavor.

~~~~~~~~~~~~~~~~~~~~~~~~~~~~~~~~~~~~~~

PREPARATION

1. Preheat the oven to 325°F. Insert liners into medium cupcake pans.

2. Prepare cupcakes: In a bowl, sift flour, baking powder, salt, ginger, cardamom and baking soda.

3. In the bowl of an electric mixer with the mixer's flat beater, cream butter and sugar on medium speed until mixture is light and fluffy.

4. Reduce mixing speed to low, add eggs one at a time, mixing well.

5. Gradually add dry ingredients (prepared in Step 2), orange juice and shredded carrots, mixing until blended into a smooth batter.

6. Fill the cupcake liners two-thirds full.

7. Bake for 20-25 minutes, or until cupcakes are springy to the touch and a toothpick inserted in cupcake's center comes out clean.

8. Remove from oven and cool on wire rack for 10 minutes.

9. Prepare frosting: With an electric mixer beat butter, cream cheese, cardamom and orange zest on low speed.

10. Gradually add powdered sugar and lemon juice, continue beating for about 2 more minutes until frosting is blended and smooth.

11. Spread frosting generously on each cupcake and serve.

Rose Cupcakes

~~~~~~~~~~~~~~~~~~~

Makes

~ *12* ~

Cupcakes

INGREDIENTS

3 cups white flour

1 tablespoon baking powder

¼ teaspoon salt

½ cup + 2½ tablespoons butter, at room temperature

¾ cup sugar

2 tablespoons rose water

3 eggs

Frosting:

1 lightly whisked egg white

3 tablespoons rose water

5 tablespoons sugar

3 cups powdered sugar

Garnish:

12 small rose buds

This is a romantic cupcake with an exotic flavor, with the rose water lending the cupcake a Oriental scent and taste. Be sure to use fresh rose water that has not been sprayed with pesticides.

~~~~~~

PREPARATION

1. Preheat the oven to 325°F. Insert liners into medium cupcake pans.

2. Prepare cupcakes: In a bowl, sift flour, baking powder and salt.

3. In the bowl of an electric mixer with the mixer's flat beater, cream butter, sugar, and rose water on medium speed until mixture is light and fluffy.

4. Reduce mixing speed to low, add eggs one at a time, mixing well.

5. Gradually add dry ingredients (prepared in Step 2) and mix until blended into a smooth batter. Fill the cupcake liners two-thirds full.

6. Bake for 20-25 minutes, or until cupcakes are springy to the touch and a toothpick inserted in cupcake's center comes out clean.

7. Remove from oven and cool on wire rack for 10 minutes.

8. Prepare frosting: In the bowl of an electric mixer, beat egg white with rose water on low speed.

9. Add sugar and powdered sugar to achieve a shiny and thick frosting.

10. Assemble: Generously spread frosting on each cupcake, garnishing with a rose bud.

Raspberry Vodka Cupcakes

~~~~~~~~~~~~~~~~~~~~

Makes

~ **12** ~

Cupcakes

INGREDIENTS

Raspberry purée:

1½ cups fresh raspberries

¾ cup powdered sugar

1 teaspoon lemon juice

Cupcakes:

3 cups white flour

1 tablespoon baking powder

¼ teaspoon salt

½ cup butter, at room temperature

1 cup sugar

2 eggs

½ cup raspberry purée

4 tablespoons raspberry flavored vodka

Frosting:

¾ cup butter, at room temperature

3¾ cups powdered sugar

3 tablespoons mascarpone cheese

Pink food coloring

4 tablespoons vodka

This is a cupcake that no one can resist. I chose to use raspberry flavored vodka to moderate the bitterness of the alcohol, but those of you unafraid to take chances are invited to experiment with various flavored vodkas, or even with classic unflavored vodka.

~~~~~~

PREPARATION

1. Prepare raspberry purée: With a fork, coarsely crush raspberries together with powdered sugar and lemon juice until a thick purée is achieved. Set aside for use in batter and as topping.

2. Preheat the oven to 325°F. Insert liners into medium cupcake pans.

3. Prepare cupcakes: In a bowl, sift flour, baking powder and salt.

4. In the bowl of an electric mixer with the mixer's flat beater, cream butter and sugar on medium speed until mixture is light and fluffy.

5. Reduce mixing speed to low, add eggs one at a time, mixing well.

6. Gradually add dry ingredients (prepared in Step 3), raspberry purée (prepared in Step 1) and vodka, mixing until blended into a smooth batter. Fill the cupcake liners two-thirds full.

7. Bake for 20-25 minutes, or until cupcakes are springy to the touch and a toothpick inserted in cupcake's center comes out clean.

8. Remove from oven and cool on wire rack for 10 minutes.

9. Prepare frosting: Cream butter, powdered sugar, and mascarpone cheese until mixture is blended.

10. Add a few drops of pink food coloring, add vodka, mix.

11. Spread a generous tablespoon of frosting on each cupcake, topping with a teaspoon of crushed raspberry purée and serve.

Plum and Port Cupcakes
~~~~~~~~~~~~~~~~~~~~

Makes
~ 12 ~
Cupcakes

INGREDIENTS

3 cups white flour

1 tablespoon baking powder

¼ teaspoon salt

½ cup butter, at room temperature

1 cup sugar

2 eggs

¼ cup port wine

½ cup sour cream

5 pitted purple plums, sliced into ½" cubes

Frosting:

¾ cup butter, at room temperature

3 tablespoons port wine

2 cups powdered sugar

Port wine perfectly complements the plums, emphasizing their sweet and sour taste.

~~~~~~~~~~~~~~~~~~~~~~~~~~~~~~~~~~

PREPARATION

1. Preheat the oven to 325°F. Insert liners into medium cupcake pans.

2. Prepare cupcakes: In a bowl, sift flour, baking powder and salt.

3. In the bowl of an electric mixer with the mixer's flat beater on medium speed, cream butter and sugar until mixture is light and fluffy.

4. Reduce mixing speed to low, add eggs one at a time, mixing well.

5. Gradually add dry ingredients (prepared in Step 2), port and sour cream, mixing well until blended into smooth batter.

6. Add cubed plums to batter and mix. Fill the cupcake liners two-thirds full.

7. Bake for 20-25 minutes, or until cupcakes are springy to the touch and a toothpick inserted in cupcake's center comes out clean.

8. Remove from oven and cool on wire rack for 10 minutes.

9. Prepare frosting: In a bowl, beat butter and port for about 1 minute.

10. Gradually add powdered sugar and mix until frosting is smooth and creamy.

11. Generously spread frosting on each cupcake and serve.

Nectarine Cupcakes

~~~~~~~~~~~~~~~~~~~

Makes

~ *12* ~

Cupcakes

INGREDIENTS

2½ cups white flour

1 tablespoon baking powder

¼ teaspoon baking soda

¼ teaspoon salt

½ cup butter, at room temperature

1½ cups sugar

2 eggs

2 tablespoons lemon juice

¾ cup sour cream

6-8 pitted nectarines, cut into cubes

Frosting:

½ cup butter, at room temperature

½ cup whipping cream

1 tablespoon vanilla extract

1⅓ cups powdered sugar

This is a fun summery recipe. The nectarines may be substituted with any sour fruit such as plums, apricots or berries.

~~~~~~

PREPARATION

1. Preheat the oven to 325°F. Insert liners into medium cupcake pans.

2. Prepare cupcakes: In a bowl, sift flour, baking powder, baking soda and salt.

3. In the bowl of an electric mixer with the mixer's flat beater on medium speed, cream butter and sugar until mixture is light and fluffy.

4. Reduce mixing speed to low, add eggs one at a time, mixing well. Add lemon juice.

5. Gradually add dry ingredients (prepared in Step 2) and sour cream, mixing until blended into smooth batter.

6. Add cubed nectarines to batter and mix. Fill the cupcake liners two-thirds full.

7. Bake for 20-25 minutes, or until cupcakes are springy to the touch and a toothpick inserted in cupcake's center comes out clean.

8. Remove from oven and cool on wire rack for 10 minutes.

9. Prepare frosting: In a bowl, cream butter for about 1 minute, add whipping cream and vanilla extract, continue beating for 1-2 minutes, add powdered sugar, mix until texture is smooth.

10. Transfer frosting into pastry bag with star tip, piping a swirl in the center of each cupcake top and serve.

Tropical Cupcakes

~~~~~~~~~~~~~~~~~~~

Makes

~ *12* ~

Cupcakes

INGREDIENTS

Mango purée:

1 fresh mango (to make ½ cup mango purée)

Cupcakes:

3 cups white flour

1 tablespoon baking powder

¼ teaspoon salt

½ cup butter, at room temperature

¾ cup sugar

2 eggs

½ cup passion fruit juice

Frosting:

½ cup butter, at room temperature

¾ cup softened cream cheese

1 tablespoon rum

3 cups powdered sugar

Garnish:

Cubed fresh mango

Fresh passion fruit seeds

This cupcake is perfect for tasting the pleasures of a Caribbean vacation. If you'd like to experience lying on the beach and eating a juicy mango bursting with flavor, this is the time to spoil yourselves with a tropical and refreshing passion fruit-mango cupcake.

~~~~~~

PREPARATION

1. Prepare mango purée: Peel and cut a fresh mango, working it into a smooth purée in a food processor.

2. Preheat the oven to 325°F. Insert liners into medium cupcake pans.

3. Prepare cupcakes: In a bowl, sift flour, baking powder and salt.

4. In the bowl of an electric mixer with the mixer's flat beater, cream butter and sugar on medium speed until mixture is light and fluffy. Reduce mixing speed to low, add eggs one at a time, mixing well.

5. In a separate bowl, combine passion fruit juice and mango purée (prepared in Step 1).

6. Gradually add dry ingredients (prepared in Step 3), half of passion fruit juice and mango purée, mixing until blended into smooth batter. Repeat step once more. Fill the cupcake liners two-thirds full.

7. Bake for 20-25 minutes, or until cupcakes are springy to the touch and a toothpick inserted in cupcake's center comes out clean.

8. Remove from oven and cool on wire rack for 10 minutes.

9. Prepare frosting: In the bowl of an electric mixer, cream butter, cream cheese, and rum on low speed for about 2 minutes until blended into smooth batter.

10. Gradually add powdered sugar continuing to cream for another 2-3 minutes to achieve a fluffy, ready to use frosting.

11. Place a generous tablespoon of cream cheese and rum frosting on each cupcake. Garnish with cubed fresh mango and fresh passion fruit seeds and serve.

Pavlova Cupcakes

~~~~~~~~~~~~~~~~~~~

Makes

~ 12 ~

Cupcakes

INGREDIENTS

2½ cups white flour

1 tablespoon baking powder

¼ teaspoon salt

½ cup butter, at room temperature

1 teaspoon pure vanilla extract

1 cup sugar

2 eggs

½ cup whole milk

Meringue:

4 egg whites

Pinch of salt

¾ cup sugar

½ cup powdered sugar

1 teaspoon cream of tartar

Besides being one of my all time favorite desserts, there is a romantic story behind the original pavlova. The tale goes that the chef who created this dessert did so in homage to his Russian ballerina lover: the whipped cream and meringue reminiscent of the dancer's tutu.

~~~~~~

PREPARATION

1. Preheat the oven to 325°F. Insert liners into medium cupcake pans.

2. Prepare cupcakes: In a bowl, sift flour, baking powder and salt.

3. In the bowl of an electric mixer with the mixer's flat beater, cream butter, vanilla extract, and sugar on medium speed until mixture is light and fluffy.

4. Reduce mixing speed to low, add eggs one at a time, mixing well.

5. Gradually add dry ingredients (prepared in Step 2) and milk, mix until blended into smooth batter. Fill the cupcake liners two-thirds full.

6. Bake for 20-25 minutes, or until cupcakes are springy to the touch, and a toothpick inserted in cupcake's center comes out clean.

7. Remove from oven and cool on wire rack for 10 minutes.

8. Prepare meringue: In the bowl of an electric mixer (the bowl must be completely dry with no traces of oil), whisk eggs and salt for about 3 minutes. (Tip: I recommend rubbing half a lemon on the bowl and then drying it. The acidity of the lemon neutralizes any trace of oil).

9. Gradually add sugar, followed by powdered sugar and finally cream of tartar. The meringue should be shiny and set.

10. Transfer batter to a pastry bag, piping kisses using a 2" tip on to a flat tray lined with baking parchment.

11. Bake for about 2 hours at 160°F, or until the meringue sets completely and easily comes off the baking paper. The low heat preserves the meringue's white color.

(continued on page 132)

(continued from page 130)

Sauce:

2½ cups fresh or frozen raspberries

½ cup powdered sugar

2 tablespoons Grand Marnier liqueur

1 tablespoon lemon juice

Whipped cream:

1 cup whipping cream

1 tablespoon vanilla extract

5 tablespoons powdered sugar

Garnish:

Fresh berries

Mint leaves

12. Prepare sauce: Blend berries in a food processor, adding powdered sugar, Grand Marnier liqueur, and lemon juice until a smooth purée is achieved.

13. Work berry purée through a dense sieve, removing berry seeds for a smooth sauce. Sauce may be kept in the freezer up to 4 months.

14. Prepare whipped cream: Whisk cream with vanilla extract and powdered sugar to achieve set cream.

15. Assemble: This dessert is assembled on a meringue base topped with cream and berries. I begin with a vanilla cupcake, upon which I build a cream tower with meringue shards (this recipe is for a classic French meringue), berry sauce and fresh berries...there is nothing better to end a romantic meal.

16. Place a heaping tablespoon of whipped cream on each cupcake, drizzle berry sauce on top of cream, garnish with meringue kisses, berries and mint leaves.

17. It is important to complete the assembly directly before serving since the meringue will lose its shape once moistened. The whipped cream will also droop after a short while.

Campari Grapefruit Cupcakes
~~~~~~~~~~~~~~~~~~~

Makes

~ 12 ~

Cupcakes

INGREDIENTS

3 cups white flour

1 tablespoon baking powder

¼ teaspoon baking soda

¼ teaspoon salt

½ cup butter, at room temperature

1 cup sugar

2 eggs

½ cup freshly squeezed red grapefruit juice

Frosting:

2 tablespoons mascarpone cheese

1 cup butter, at room temperature

2 cups powdered sugar

3 tablespoons Campari

Garnish:

Red grapefruit segments, sliced into three

Campari is a liqueur made from more than 60 herbs and plants, is red in color and bitter-sweet in flavor. The especially winning cocktail combination of campari and red grapefruit juice also works wonderfully in the following cupcake recipe.
~~~~~~

PREPARATION

1. Preheat the oven to 325°F. Insert liners into medium cupcake pans.

2. Prepare cupcakes: In a bowl, sift flour, baking powder, baking soda and salt.

3. In the bowl of an electric mixer with the mixer's flat beater, cream butter and sugar on medium speed until mixture is light and fluffy.

4. Reduce mixing speed to low, add eggs one at a time, mixing well.

5. Gradually add dry ingredients (prepared in Step 2) and grapefruit juice, mix until smooth batter is achieved. Fill the cupcake liners two-thirds full.

6. Bake for 20-25 minutes, or until cupcakes are springy to the touch and a toothpick inserted in cupcake's center comes out clean.

7. Remove from oven and cool on wire rack for 10 minutes.

8. Prepare frosting: With an electric mixer, cream mascarpone and butter on low speed for about 2 minutes.

9. Gradually add powdered sugar and Campari, continuing to cream for 2-3 more minutes until frosting is light and fluffy.

10. Top cupcakes with Campari frosting, garnish with red grapefruit segments and serve.

Pistachio and White Chocolate Cupcakes
~~~~~~~~~~~~~~~~~~~~

Makes

~ *12* ~

Cupcakes

INGREDIENTS

3 cups white flour

1 tablespoon baking powder

¼ teaspoon salt

½ cup butter, at room temperature

1 cup sugar

4 tablespoons pistachio purée

2 eggs

½ cup sour cream

Frosting:

⅔ cup white chocolate, broken into cubes

½ cup butter, at room temperature

¾ cup softened cream cheese

2 tablespoons pistachio purée

2 cups powdered sugar

Garnish:

White chocolate shavings

The flavor and color of these cupcakes is mostly derived from the pistachio purée - which is why it's so important to purchase high quality purée (I usually buy a French-made purée). Once you've got a good purée, half the work is done. In combination with the white chocolate, the pistachio cupcake is a stylish and splendid dessert, worthy of being served at the end of an elegant meal.
~~~~~~

PREPARATION

1. Preheat the oven to 325°F. Insert liners into medium cupcake pans.

2. Prepare cupcakes: In a bowl, sift flour, baking powder and salt.

3. In the bowl of an electric mixer with the mixer's flat beater, cream butter, sugar, and pistachio purée on medium speed until mixture is light and fluffy.

4. Reduce mixing speed to low, add eggs one at a time, mixing well.

5. Gradually add dry ingredients (prepared in Step 2) and sour cream, mixing until blended into smooth batter. Fill the cupcake liners two-thirds full.

6. Bake for 20-25 minutes, or until cupcakes are springy to the touch and a toothpick inserted in cupcake's center comes out clean.

7. Remove from oven and cool on wire rack for 10 minutes.

8. Prepare frosting: In a bowl placed over a pot of hot water (double boiler), melt white chocolate, mixing until texture is blended. Remove from heat and cool for about 5 minutes.

9. In the bowl of an electric mixer, cream butter, cream cheese, and pistachio purée on low speed for about 2 minutes until texture is blended and smooth.

10. Gradually pour in melted white chocolate and powdered sugar, continuing to beat for 2-3 minutes until frosting is blended, fluffy and ready to use.

11. Spread a generous tablespoon on each cupcake, sprinkling white chocolate shavings on top and serve.

Upside-Down Apple Tatin Cupcakes

~~~~~~~~~~~~~~~~~~

Makes
~ 12 ~
Cupcakes

INGREDIENTS

Caramelized apples:

3 small Granny Smith apples

¾ cup sugar

2 tablespoons butter, at room temperature

2 tablespoons heavy cream, at room temperature

Cupcakes:

3 cups white flour

1 tablespoon baking powder

¼ teaspoon salt

½ cup butter, at room temperature

1 cup sugar

1 teaspoon vanilla extract

2 eggs

1½ cups buttermilk

This is a classic cake that has been altered to fit the cupcake mold. After baking, cupcakes are turned upside down, allowing the caramelized apple juices to seep in and moisten the spongy dough of the cupcakes.

~~~~~~

PREPARATION

1. Prepare caramelized apples: Peel, seed and slice apples into small pieces.

2. In a saucepan on low heat, melt sugar until a light and delicate caramel is formed.

3. Keeping pan away from body, carefully add butter and cream, mixing with a wooden spoon to create toffee caramel. To prevent lumps in the sauce, make sure that neither ingredient is cold.

4. Add apples and cook on low heat for about 4 minutes to soften.

5. Once apples are soft, remove from heat and cool completely.

6. Preheat the oven to 325°F. Insert liners into medium cupcake pans.

7. Prepare cupcakes: In a bowl, sift flour, baking powder and salt.

8. In the bowl of an electric mixer with the mixer's flat beater, cream butter, sugar, and vanilla extract on medium speed until mixture is light and fluffy.

9. Reduce mixing speed to low, add eggs one at a time, mixing well.

10. Gradually add dry ingredients (prepared in Step 7) and buttermilk, mixing until blended into smooth batter.

11. Fill the cupcake liners: Place cooled, caramelized apples at bottom of each muffin liner (4-5 pieces each), thoroughly coat each bottom with a teaspoon of caramel sauce.

12. Fill the cupcake liners two-thirds full with batter.

13. Bake 20-25 minutes, or until cupcakes are springy to the touch and a toothpick inserted in cupcake's center comes out clean.

(continued on page 138)

(continued from page 136)

14. Remove and cool on wire rack for about 5 minutes (cooling too long risks causing the caramel to harden and the apple pieces will then stick to the muffin tins).

15. Use your fingers to pull out the cupcake, turning it upside down 180 degrees and setting it on a plate with the apples facing up. Make sure the hot caramel liquid does not drip on your hands.

16. Gently lift off the paper liners. A tasty addition when serving these cupcakes hot out of the oven is crème fraiche.

Vanilla Cream Puff Cupcakes
~~~~~~~~~~~~~~~~~~

Makes
~ 10 ~
Cream puffs

INGREDIENTS

1 cup milk

7 tablespoons butter, at room temperature

½ tablespoon sugar

½ tablespoon salt

1 cup white flour

4 eggs

1 egg for glaze

This is actually a classic French recipe for vanilla filled cream puffs with powdered sugar...not exactly a cupcake, but certainly a personal, cupcake sized treat. To make your cream puffs even more exciting, drizzle chocolate syrup on top of the ready cream puff, or add additional flavors to the vanilla filling such as coffee, chocolate, and dulce de leche.
~~~~~~~~~~~~~~~~~~~~~~~~~~~~~~~~~~

PREPARATION

1. Preheat the oven to 375°F. Insert liners into medium cupcake pans.

2. Prepare cream puffs: In a saucepan, heat milk, butter, sugar and salt just to boiling. Remove from heat.

3. Add flour to the liquids, mixing rapidly with a wooden spoon until wet dough is achieved.

4. Return dough to pot (to dry any liquids), mixing for about 1 minute until mixture is no longer sticky.

5. Transfer warm dough to the bowl of an electric mixer, adding eggs one at a time, mixing well until blended.

Filling:

1 vanilla bean

4 cups milk

2 cups sugar

8 egg yolks

½ cup corn flour

Garnish:

Powdered sugar

6. Transfer dough to a pastry bag with a round tip. Fill the cupcake liners three-fourths full.

7. Whisk remaining egg with 2 tablespoons water and brush on cream puffs.

8. Bake for about 20 minutes.

9. Prepare filling: Slice vanilla bean in half and scrape insides with a knife.

10. In a saucepan, heat milk with scraped out vanilla beans and half the sugar.

11. In a bowl, whisk egg yolks with remaining sugar, add corn flour.

12. When the milk boils, pour a small amount into egg mixture and mix. Repeat this step twice.

13. Return mixture to pot and continue cooking on low heat, while stirring constantly, until texture is thick and creamy. Remove from heat and cool.

15. Transfer cooled vanilla cream to a pastry bag with a narrow (#5) tip.

16. With the point of the tip, create a hole in the base of each cream puff and fill with vanilla cream.

17. When cream comes out of hole slightly, you will know that the cream puff is full.

18. Sprinkle with powdered sugar before serving. Cream puffs will keep in refrigerator for up to 3 days.

Conversion Charts

~~~~~~

The exact equivalents in the following charts have been rounded up for convenience.

Dry/Liquid Measures

~~~~~~~~~~~~~~~~~~~~~~~

U.S.	Metric
¼ teaspoon	1.25 milliliters
½ teaspoon	2 milliliters
1 teaspoon	5 milliliters
1 tablespoon (3 teaspoons)	15 milliliters
1 fluid ounce (2 tablespoons)	30 milliliters
¼ cup	60 milliliters
⅓ cup	80 milliliters
½ cup	120 milliliters
1 cup	240 milliliters

Length

~~~~~~~~~~~~~~~~~~~~

U.S.	Metric
¼ inch	3 millimeters
¼ inch	6 millimeters
½ inch	12 millimeters
1 inch	2.5 centimeters

Oven Temperature

~~~~~~~~~~~~~~~~~~~~~~~

Degrees Fahrenheit	Degrees Celsius	Gas Mark	Description
225	110	¼	Very slow
250	120/130	½	Very slow
275	140	1	Slow
300	150	2	Slow
325	160/170	3	Moderate
350	180	4	Moderate
375	190	5	Moderately hot
400	200	6	Moderately hot
425	220	7	Hot
450	230	8	Hot
475	240	9	Very hot

Cup Measures

~~~~~~~~~~~~~~~~~~~~

1 cup almonds, flaked	110 grams	3½ ounces
1 cup almonds, slivered	170 grams	5½ ounces
1 cup apricots, dried	190 grams	6½ ounces
1 cup blueberries, fresh	125 grams	4 ounces
1 cup blueberries, frozen	125 grams	4 ounces
1 cup carrots, grated	115 grams	3½ ounces
1 cup chocolate, chopped	150 grams	5 ounces
1 cup cocoa powder	115 grams	3½ ounces
1 cup double cream (thick)	250 grams	8 ounces
1 cup dates, chopped	160 grams	5½ ounces
1 cup flour, plain	135 grams	4½ ounces
1 cup golden syrup	380 grams	13 ounces
1 cup hazelnuts, whole	130 grams	4 ounces
1 cup honey	400 grams	14 ounces
1 cup confectioner's (icing) sugar	125 grams	4 ounces
1 cup maple syrup	380 grams	1½ ounces
1 cup pecans, chopped	110 grams	3½ ounces
1 cup poppy seeds	150 grams	5 ounces
1 cup raisins	200 grams	7 ounces
1 cup raspberries, fresh	125 grams	4 ounces
1 cup raspberries, frozen	125 grams	4 ounces
1 cup sour cream	250 grams	8 ounces
1 cup sugar, brown	200 grams	7 ounces
1 cup sugar, caster (superfine)	225 grams	7½ ounces
1 cup sugar, white	225 grams	7½ ounces
1 cup thick (double) cream	250 grams	8 ounces

Index

~~~~~~~~~~~~~~~~~~~~

A

allspice, 90

almond

almond extract, 36, 72, 91, 92, 120

almond flour, 77, 120

anise stars, 90

Anniversary Mini Cinnamon Cupcakes, 78

apples, 26, 136, 138

apple cider, 26

Apple-Cinnamon Cupcakes, 26

apricot

apricot jam, 92

apricot neutral glaze, 92

B

Baby Shower Cupcakes, 68

baking powder, 10, 13, 14, 16, 21, 24, 26, 27, 28, 31, 32, 34, 36, 37, 38, 40, 41, 42, 48, 50, 52, 53, 54, 56, 58, 60, 62, 64, 68, 70, 72, 74, 76, 78, 80, 82, 86, 88, 90, 91, 92, 94, 96, 97, 98, 100, 102, 103, 104, 106, 108, 109, 112, 115, 116, 118, 120, 121, 122, 124, 126, 127, 128, 130, 133, 134, 136

baking soda, 13, 14, 16, 21, 24, 25, 26, 27, 28, 31, 32, 36, 37, 40, 41, 42, 48, 56, 60, 62, 64, 68, 72, 74, 76, 77, 78, 80, 82, 86, 91, 96, 97, 102, 103, 121, 127, 133

balsamic vinegar, 25

banana, 38

Banana Chocolate Cupcakes, 38

Basic Recipes, 12

Black and White Sesame Cupcakes, 103

Black Forest Cupcakes, 31

blueberries, 40, 44

Blueberry Cupcakes with Vanilla Cream, 40

bowl and mixing spoon, 9

brandy, 60, 61, 80

butter, 10

Buttercream Frosting, 17

buttermilk, 13, 14, 52, 56, 68, 77, 90, 100, 112, 116, 136

C

Campari, 133

Campari Grapefruit Cupcakes, 133

candies, 52, 70, 72, 74

candy sprinkles, 52, 70

Caramel Sundae Cupcakes, 53

cardamom, 121

Carrot, Ginger and Cardamom Cupcakes, 121

Cellophane paper, 56

chamomile tea, 37

Chestnut Cupcakes, 76

chestnut purée, 76

chocolate, 12, 13, 14, 17, 31, 32, 36, 38, 42, 44, 53, 54, 56, 60, 61, 74, 86, 96, 103, 116, 134, 138

Chocolate Chip Cupcakes, 36

Chocolate Ganache, 12

Chocolate Mint Cupcakes, 32

Chocolate Mousse Madness Cupcakes, 60

Classic Chocolate Cupcakes, 13

cinnamon, 26, 27, 28, 30, 78, 90, 94, 102

cloves, 78, 102

cocoa, 13, 17, 31, 42, 56, 60, 86, 115

cocoa powder, 13, 17, 56, 86, 115

coconut, 41, 68, 88, 94

Coconut Cupcakes, 41

coffee beans, 118

Coffee Whiskey Cupcakes, 118

Colorful Candies, 10

cookie cutters, 80

corn

corn flour, 10, 40, 91, 112

corn syrup, 36

Craft Project Cupcakes, 52

cream cheese, 15, 38, 41, 42, 44, 58, 68, 70, 78, 80, 103, 104, 121, 128, 134

Cream Cheese Frosting, 15

cream of tartar, 19, 116, 130, 132

Crème Brulée Cupcakes, 112

crème fraiche, 72, 80, 138

crystal sugar, 68

D

Dairy-free Cupcakes, 16

decorations, 10

demerara sugar, 112

dulce de leche, 76, 138

E

eggs, 10

Egg White Royal Frosting, 15

equipment, 9

espresso, 115, 118

F

flax seeds, 108

flour, 10

Fondant Glaze, 18

food coloring, 10, 52, 68, 78, 82, 97, 102, 124

G

ginger, 21, 27, 121

    Ginger Orange Cupcakes, 21

    Gingerbread Cupcakes, 27

gluten, 18, 64, 77, 106

    Gluten and Dairy Free Cupcakes, 91

    Gluten Free Passover Cupcakes, 77

golden syrup, 10, 27

gooseberries, 98

    Gooseberry and Pumpkin Seed Cupcakes, 98

graham crackers, 44

Granola Cupcakes, 94

green tea, 97

    Green Tea Cupcakes, 97

grenadine, 104

H

hazelnut

    hazelnut powder, 100

    Hazelnut-Honey Cupcakes, 100

honey 10, 37, 58, 94, 100, 108

    Honey Cupcakes for Winnie the Pooh, 37

K

Kahlua, 86, 115

kirsch, 31

L

lavender, 102

Lavender, Clove and Cinnamon Cupcakes, 102

Lemon, 18, 19, 34, 96

    Lemon Cupcakes, 34

    Lemon Frosting, 18

    lemon juice, 15, 18, 19, 21, 27, 34, 80, 91, 96, 97, 102, 104, 121, 124, 127, 130, 132

    Lemon Yogurt Cupcakes, 96

lollipop

    Lollipop Cupcakes, 56

    lollipop sticks, 56

M

M & M's, 52

macadamia nuts, 109

mandarin, 21, 22

mango, 128

maple

    maple syrup, 10, 24, 28, 53, 106

    Maple-Pecan Cupcakes, 24

maraschino cherries, 31

Marble Cupcakes, 42

marshmallows, 62

marzipan, 120

    Marzipan Cupcakes, 120

mascarpone, 28, 30, 37, 52, 72, 100, 115, 124, 133

measuring tools, 9

Meringue Frosting, 19

Mini Chocolate Valentine Cupcakes, 74

Mini Mascarpone Birthday Cupcakes, 72

Mini-Me Marshmallow Cupcakes, 62

mint, 32, 78, 82, 132

molasses, 10, 94, 98

N

nectarines, 127

    Nectarine Cupcakes, 127

New York Cheese Cupcakes, 44

nutmeg, 27, 38, 82, 88

O

oatmeal, 94

    Oatmeal-Macadamia Nut Cupcakes, 109

orange juice, 21, 121

Oreo Cupcakes, 50

oven, 9

P

pacifiers, 68

pans, 9

passion fruit, 128

pastry bags, 10

Pavlova Cupcakes, 130

peanuts, 53

    peanut butter, 58

    Peanut Butter and Jelly Cupcakes, 58

Pear Crumble Cupcakes, 28

pears, 28

pecans, 24

peppermint extract, 32

pistachio

    Pistachio and White Chocolate Cupcakes, 134

pistachio purée, 134

Plum and Port Cupcakes, 126

pomegranate, 104

    Pomegranate Cupcakes, 104

poppy seed, 92

    Poppy Seed Cupcakes, 92

port wine, 126

potato flour, 10, 77

powdered sugar, 15, 17, 19, 21, 25, 27, 28, 30, 31, 34, 37, 38, 41, 42, 44, 52, 60, 61, 62, 68, 70, 72, 76, 77, 78, 80, 82, 86, 91, 97, 100, 102, 104, 121, 122, 124, 126, 127, 128, 130, 132, 133, 134, 138, 139

Powdered Sugar and Lemon Glaze, 19

pumpkin

    Pumpkin Cupcakes, 82

    pumpkin seeds, 98

Q

Quaker oats, 109

quinoa, 106

    Quinoa-Walnut Cupcakes, 106

R

raisins, 90, 94

raspberry

    Raspberry Vodka Cupcakes, 124

    raspberries, 124, 130

    raspberry purée, 124

rose

    Rose Cupcakes, 122

    rose petals, 34, 122

    rose water, 122

rum extract, 48

S

semolina, 90

Semolina and Raisin Cupcakes, 90

sesame seeds, 103, 108

sour cream, 32, 44, 62, 74, 78, 126, 127, 134

soy milk, 91, 103

storage suggestions, 10

strawberries, 25

    strawberry jam, 48, 58

    strawberry preserves, 48

    strawberry sorbet, 48

Strawberry Shortcake Cupcakes, 25

Strawberry Surprise Cupcakes with Strawberry Sorbet, 48

sugar crystal, 34, 52, 68

sugar dough, 10

sunflower seeds, 94

T

tahini, 108

    Tahini, Linseed and Date Honey Cupcakes, 108

tangerine, 21

tapioca flour, 77, 91

tartar powder, 19

thermometer, 18

thin sieve/sifter, 9

timer, 9

Tiramisu Cupcakes, 115

Toffee Square Cupcake Surprise, 64

Top Hat Cupcakes, 116

Triple Chocolate Knockout Cupcakes, 54

Tropical Cupcakes, 128

U

Upside-Down Apple Tatin Cupcakes, 136

V

vanilla bean, 112, 139

Vanilla Cream Puff Cupcakes, 138

Vanilla Cupcakes, 14

vanilla extract, 13, 14, 15, 16, 17, 25, 28, 36, 37, 40, 41, 42, 52, 53, 56, 62, 68, 70, 72, 74, 77, 90, 91, 98, 100, 103, 112, 116, 127, 130, 132, 136

vanilla ice cream, 28, 53

Vegan Dark Chocolate Cupcakes, 86

W

Wedding Cupcakes, 70

whipping cream, 12, 24, 25, 31, 32, 44, 53, 54, 60, 64, 74, 127, 130

whiskey, 118

White Christmas Cupcakes, 80

Whole Wheat Hazelnut Cupcakes, 88

wire cooling rack, 10

Y

yogurt, 96